The Hanging Gardens of Babylon

ISMAIEL ALDEAN
EDITED BY ROSE ALDEAN

Copyright © 2011 Ismaiel Aldean
All rights reserved.

ISBN: 1466428198
ISBN 13: 9781466428195

THE HANGING GARDENS OF BABYLON

To Mary, my wife and dearest friend. For your self-denial and dedication to our family over the last 42 years and going. Without you, we would not have made it to where we are today.

And to Marwan; you are always in our thoughts.

This book is for you.

Acknowledgements

I would like to express my deepest love and appreciation to my daughter Rose for her consistent encouragement and for pushing me to write down my life stories. Her tireless efforts and input made it possible for me to contemplate publishing it.

A very big fatherly love and thanks to my youngest son Muzzi for his constructive comments and for reviewing the manuscript.

Many thanks to my dear friend David Meek, for his continuous support and advice right from the start; his experienced eye provided us with the most valuable feedback and helped shape the book.

I would also like to thank Ms Liz Costello, my colleague at Spire Hospital Manchester, for the many hours she spent typing the manuscript, taking up her precious time away from her family.

Thank you to all my friends and family, who have been on this journey with me and particularly those who helped me through the hardest times.

Last and not least my sincere thanks to my friend, who knocked on my door more than two decades ago; I doubt you will ever know the true impact you had on my life. Without you, I dread to think of the suffering we would have endured; I cannot thank you enough.

INTRODUCTION

Many people might wonder why I have waited this long to write down my life experiences from Iraq; Saddam has been gone a few years now and it has been relatively safe to uncover some old truths. Well, in short, this is how the book came about.

When we left Iraq in the summer of 1990, Rose my youngest daughter was 3 years old. My son Muzzi was born in England in 1992; so both of them missed out on our life in Iraq.

Rose, for whatever reason, grew up very much attached to her Iraqi roots, yet she was too young to remember any places or faces. Whenever we reminisced as a family, about life back home, Rose always felt left out and upset that she couldn't relate to our stories. Her feelings really surfaced when we brought out family photographs and she would ask me about family and friends. When she saw pictures of herself, her sisters and Mary and I sat in our garden surrounded by bodyguards, she would call me 'The Godfather'.

She would always ask about what life was like for us in Iraq and why we left; the response I gave was always a half truth, and as she grew older she knew that there was something missing from the stories. Not until recent years, when I felt she was old enough, did I tell her about what really happened and how we ended up in the UK with nothing but two suitcases.

I always thought her link with Iraq would gradually fade away, but to the contrary she became more interested and attached to the family we left behind. She impressively picked up the Iraqi language that she had once forgotten as a child and always stayed true to the Iraqi culture.

It was on a lovely summer evening in June 2009, when the whole family were relaxing in our pool in Cyprus; we had been talking about Iraq and laughing at what the girls could remember from their childhood. We talked and admired the sunset over the ocean; a time that, in Iraqi tradition, your prayers to God are answered. As I was saying my usual prayer of thanks to God for everything we have, I remember Rose coming out of the blue with 'I think you should write a book about your life.'

I laughed it off and thought it was ridiculous that anybody be interested in my life, I didn't think it was anything worth writing about. But then all the children began to support her idea; saying that whenever their friends find out they are from Iraq, they ask stories about what life was like, what it was like to live under Saddam; stories which Rose and Muzzi at least, were unable to tell without finding out more from me.

It wasn't the first time Rose had asked me to do this, but this time it felt more heartfelt and serious. She said that if I didn't want to write a book, she at least wanted me to write down some of my memoires in a diary so that she had stories to tell her children about their grandparents.

That night I just couldn't sleep. I started to think about what the children had been saying about my life and the fact that maybe I owed it to them to bare some of the truth. I lay wide awake for a few hours, until eventually at 4 a.m. I went out onto the balcony and started writing.

Once pen touched paper, an unbelievable replay of my life appeared. It was an enjoyable, addictive and effortless process of translating my memories into written words. It brought up times from the past that I had suppressed on purpose, as well as times I had simply forgotten about. It made me realise that perhaps some of my experiences were more unusual than I thought.

By Christmas 2009, I handed Rose my written memoires in a scrap book. For her or her children, I had put down in raw words, some of the most memorable moments of my life. Within days she had finished reading over 130,000 words and decided that she would make it into a book, regardless of whether I thought people would be interested.

Two years on, this is the final product.

PREFACE

I was born in Baghdad on September 21st 1946 in a British nursing home; the third and youngest boy in the family, to be followed only by my sister four years later.

My father was a highly educated man and a successful lawyer, having studied in Iraq, Syria, Egypt and France. When he passed away in 1995, he had taught us a great deal about life; how to keep going when times were hard and the importance of family relationships.

My mother was a housewife, an excellent mother whom we respected immensely. She read extensively and was self educated.

My eldest brother, Ibrahim, studied Economics and Commerce at the University of Baghdad and spent his career in the Financial Sector; for the last fifteen years of his working life he was the Managing Director of Al Rashid Bank. Ibrahim passed away unexpectedly two years ago.

My other brother, Ahmed, was initially called to military service for a teaching and administrative job, but soon after starting he was forced to become more deeply involved in the army as a high-ranking officer. In such a position, he witnessed all of the horrors generated by Saddam's internal and external wars.

My only sister, Anwar, graduated from university with a Bachelors Degree in French and English. She went on to become Assistant Managing Director of a large textile company in Babylon.

As for me, I developed an early passion for medicine and decided at a young age to become a surgeon. I have been a Doctor for the past forty-five years. I do not remember any times of hardship when growing up; we were a close family and my memories of childhood are happy ones.

My family was one of the most famous and highly respected families in Iraq; we are direct descendants of Prophet Mohammed and as such are known as *Sayed* (Master).

When Saddam Hussein came to power, he requested information about the predominant tribes that made up the social structure of Iraq. He ordered his government officers to research and draw up a family tree for every significant family in Iraq. My family tree was one of the first to be presented to Saddam. It was officially certified and to this day remains framed in my family home.

Following medical school, I decided to go to England for surgical training and during my time at New Cross Hospital, Wolverhampton, I met my wife Mary. To be certain she could cope with life in Iraq, I arranged for her to visit home and live with my parents for a few weeks. She fell in love with the country and the people. We were married in 1975. In 1978, whilst working on the Isle of Wight, we decided to go back to Iraq. We lived in Iraq for twelve years, raised five children and lived through the Iran/Iraq war.

Ismaiel Aldean

Due to my family background and my position in society, I witnessed and experienced things that even many Iraqi people were unaware of ever happening. This book is comprised of my memories of the most significant events that occurred both before and during Saddam Hussein's dictatorship. These events not only changed my life but also provided me with a rare insight into the mind of Saddam Hussein and the grip that he held over my country. I hope that this account of my experiences enable you to understand the difficulties still surrounding Iraq and its people.

Ismaiel, October 2011, Cheshire, UK

Note:
This book recalls my life story and real events that I experienced both directly and through family and friends; the names of people, places and dates have been changed throughout.

→ This was the same hospital that I was taken into with a suspected fracture of the spin. I was given an injection straight away by the Ward Sister - Betty M°Goldrick. & then we got married 1½ yrs later on our joint birthday - 29/6/1963

Ron Bissett

THE KNOCK

Whilst in Iraq, I established myself as a successful surgeon with both public and private clinics across the country. I built my own hospital in Babylon, which was named after me, and was completed in 1988. On reflection, I can see clearly that my life in Iraq at this time was in its prime. Not only was I surrounded by close family and friends but I was showered with respect for the valued service I provided for the community. At that time we lived in the lap of luxury, I was able to provide my family with whatever they desired; we had everything from luxurious houses and maids, to private chauffeurs and lavish holidays.

These were probably the best years of my life. I can picture in my mind as though it were yesterday the typical evening at home; with family and friends relaxing at my orchard, the smell of home cooked food and the comforting sound of my children, nieces and nephews playing around my feet.

The relationships I developed while back home not only helped me to live quite comfortably in Iraq, but also eventually became the very reason I made it out alive. Following the eight year Iran Iraq war, I was frequently advised by some of the most high-ranking government officials to leave the country. At the time I took it as a kind gesture from close friends who cared about me and my family, rather than serious advice to leave.

That was until a hot summer evening in 1990, when there was a knock on my door. A very close friend of mine had come to see me. He was no ordinary acquaintance; he was part of Saddam's inner circle. I knew from the moment that he stepped into my house that this was not a social call. Without the usual chit-chat, he told me that I needed to leave Iraq immediately. I could see the concern and panic on his face; I sensed the urgency in his voice and that he knew something he couldn't share with me.

'There is an imminent threat, Ismaiel,' he said. 'If you don't leave now you will regret it for the rest of your life. Think of your girls, your wife. You have to think of their future, it is no longer your own.'

'When are you talking about?' I asked. 'A month, two months?'

'Tomorrow, Doctor. You have to leave tomorrow.'

The tremble in his voice was well contained, as expected from any such high ranking officer. The message was clear and it didn't take much to realise that this time, it was more than a gentle reminder, it was a definite warning. I wanted to ask questions but knew better than to delve into the secrets of Saddam's circle. I knew what I had to do and was prepared to give everything up to do so.

IN THE BEGINNING

Although competition was fierce, in 1963 I got a place at Baghdad University Medical School. I was thrilled and realised this was the first step in conquering my childhood dream of being a Doctor. It was one of the most prestigious schools in Iraq, having been established by the British in 1921, and I felt privileged to be there.

Whilst in Baghdad I lived with my brothers, who were also studying at the University, and we rented a three bedroom flat in a place called *Al Adhamya*. The medical school accepted an average of two hundred students each year, attracting applicants from all over the country. The majority of my fellow classmates were from middle and upper-class families, as the cost of education was very high at the time.

We were taught medicine in the English language and most of our lecturers were British. At first, studying in English proved to be a bit of a struggle; first year topics covered complicated terminology across physics, chemistry, biology and maths. Through hard work and determination, I began to master the English language and managed to pass my first year exams at the first sitting.

In the following two years, the work became harder and was much more focused around anatomy, physiology,

The Hanging Gardens of Babylon

pathology and histology. For all medical students, dealing with a dead body for the first time is probably the hardest part of the course, which is why anatomy was the biggest challenge for us all.

We were divided into groups of eight and each group was allocated a cadaver, which had a bracelet around the wrist to indicate the number of the group. All of the cadavers were immersed in a huge well of formaldehyde in order to preserve the tissue. At the start of every practical anatomy session, we were ordered to place a plastic apron over our white coats, glove our hands and go to the well to fish for our allocated dead body.

To this day, the sharp distinctive smell of the formaldehyde and rotting flesh that filled the Anatomy Hall turns my stomach. We would pick up a long hook and dip it into the well, fishing for our allocated corpse. If we had the wrong one, we would have to let it drop back down to the depths of the well, and repeat this process until we had the correct body.

At first it was disturbing to watch the empty shell, of a once living being, lie in the silence of the formaldehyde along with others like it. The use of the cold hook and numbered bracelets also added to the eerie, inhumane feeling of this process. When we eventually succeeded in getting our allocated cadaver, we would lay it on a dissecting bench, get our dissecting tools and scalpels, open our books and take turns to dissect. Luckily I had five girls in my group who didn't want to get their hands dirty and I would always volunteer to do it on their behalf. It was an excellent learning opportunity and really sparked my interest in surgery.

During the first part of the academic year we progressed very slowly through the anatomy and dissection of the body. We ran out of time just before our Finals and were unable to dissect the head and brain. This was one of the most crucial parts of our syllabus and also extremely important to learn for our clinical career. I pleaded with the Head of the Department to give us extended access to the Anatomy Hall, without success. The school was tough and refused to grant any extra time, we knew that if we didn't cover the head and the brain we were sure to fail the entire year.

I was not prepared to fail the year and decided to take things into my own hands. I knew that in my own time I could easily dissect the head and neck in less than a week. At the end of our final anatomy session, I secretly removed the head from our cadaver and wrapped it in my white coat to take home. I returned the rest of the body to the well and rushed out of the school. At this point in time I had dealt with the bodies so frequently that the thought of carrying a man's head home didn't even faze me.

It was about 5pm when I got to the bus stop. It was absolutely heaving with people who had just finished work and were sheltering in the shade from the sweltering Iraqi sun. I must have become immune to that once pungent stench of the formaldehyde and dead bodies, because as soon as I stood in the queue, everybody around me began to disperse. It was the first and last time that I didn't have to fight the crowd to get on the bus. In fact, not one person from that stop boarded the bus with me. The few passengers already on the bus quickly got off at the following stop, all but one old couple, who kept gazing over with disapproving eyes at me whilst covering their noses with their Arabic headwear.

I was relieved when the bus finally approached my stop at *Al Adhamya*, but as I was trying to balance all my books in my right hand and the head in my left, I suddenly lost grip of the white coat. The head slipped out of the coat in what felt like slow motion, and fell to the floor with a dull thud before rolling towards the driver. I didn't want to make eye contact with the old couple, or the bus driver, but I was sure they were too scared to comment.

It wasn't until that moment that I realised how horrific the site of the head must have been to strangers; I had become numbed to the fact that I was dealing with a real human body part. I suddenly felt ashamed about the way I had gone about this but didn't expect them to give me the time of day to explain myself, so wrapped it back up and ran down the side street.

Back at our flat I was terrified of my older brothers coming back from lectures and finding the head of a dead man in their home. I hid the head in a box under my bed, and heavily sprayed the flat with deodorant, hoping to cover up the smell of formaldehyde. When my brothers came home they were appalled by the blatant stench. I quickly admitted to my brothers what had happened and tried to explain why I had done it, before I got into any further trouble. Both my brothers were too scared to even look at the head and they went to live with my Aunt until my home tuition phase was over.

I kept it for a total of five days; the rest of my group joining me on the roof of my flat where we worked on it for up to seven hours a day. Within three days I had mastered that part of the body well and to this day I know the anatomy of a head like the back of my hand. I returned the head in the same way I took it and released it to the seemingly bottomless formaldehyde well.

Nobody ever questioned the headless body and its corresponding counterpart in the formaldehyde well. I came top of the class in the anatomy finals and in October 1968, I graduated from medical school.

MILITARY SERVICE

Following graduation I had to face military service, a mandatory requirement for all young men in Iraq. The first training camp was called the Reserve Army College, where I was ranked as a Private for four months before qualifying as a Medical Lieutenant. The Reserve Army College was part of a large extensive military camp called Al Rashid; it spread over an area of nearly 100km^2 in West Baghdad.

From the first day, we learnt the hard way. Army training was purposefully strict to teach us extreme self-discipline and tolerance for life hardship. We were taught to live in very rough conditions and trained to fight and survive a war; unfortunately, most of my comrades would have to put such skills to use some day. Every day was a strict routine, waking up at 5am and going to sleep at 6pm. Food was served at a set time once a day and we could not begin eating until we heard a whistle blow. This routine was strenuous at the start, but the sickening thing is that it became normality; our bodies began to respond to routine and function almost robotically to the times set for us. We slept when we were told, we ate when we were told and we washed when we were told.

In the army you learn very fast not to argue. It was drummed into us that we had no rights and that we were there to serve our country; mere tools in the divine plan of the state. It was simple. If you stepped out of line, you would be punished, hard. Our punishments were subject directly to the will of the Corporals. Our misfortune, for relatively insignificant acts of defiance, was heavily dependent on their moods. It could involve standing immersed up to your neck in dirty, disease-infested waters for over twelve hours. It could involve putting a heavy weight, usually a car wheel, on your back and being forced to crawl for five hundred metres on your hands and feet.

One winter we made a joke about the Corporal who was teaching us to dismantle a gun. We spent entire night marching without rest; some of the other men had fallen to their knees with exhaustion, only to be punished further.

There was never any free time in the military. If you were lucky enough to know somebody you would get a one-hour pass out of the camp. One hour would get you exactly nowhere, and they knew it.

After two months of military service I had had enough, so I decided to break out of the camp with one of my close friends, to go out in Baghdad for the night. We waited for silence to drown out the barracks. Once quiet filled the room we tiptoed around, stuffing pillows under our blankets to make it appear as if we were fast asleep in bed; the oldest trick in the book. The main gate to the camp was heavily guarded, and we knew that we would probably have been shot without a second thought if we tried to escape this way.

Knowing that the boundaries of the camp were bordered with electric fencing we decided to dig a hole underneath and escape like the very animals we were treated like. Once on the other side we breathed in the fresh air and tasted freedom. It tasted good. We started to walk towards the main road, which was within the camp boundaries, and attempted to hitchhike into Baghdad. It wasn't long before a car appeared but it drove on without stopping for us.

Suddenly I heard a car coming from the opposite direction; it was the same car reversing all the way up the road to stop for us. We had hit the jackpot; a beautiful black Chevrolet pulled up and offered to take us into the city. We both clambered into the front and sat next to the quiet driver; an emotionless face, only characterised by his handle-bar moustache. There was a robust figure of a man sitting in the back, but merely a silhouette in the darkness of the Chevrolet.

'Where are you going?' the silhouette questioned.

'We want to go to the city, we've had enough of the gruelling regime and we need to get out,' I quickly replied.

He stayed silent for a moment before replying: 'And what do you plan to do in the city?'

'We want to get out of here and have some fun, see some friends, eat some good food and relax.'

He laughed out loud and asked us how we managed to get out of the camp. Proud of our efforts, my friend began to explain how we had mastered the escape whilst avoiding the watchful eye of the Corporals.

'Very clever, boys' the man responded. 'And what about your beds in a late night inspection?'

'Easy,' my friend answered, 'we put our pillows under the covers so it looks like we are still there. Generally the

Corporals who check on us at night are half-asleep and so stupid they'd never look twice.'

By this point we had reached a big roundabout and the driver took us down an exit marked: 'Private – No Entry'. Thinking that he had not noticed his mistake, I leaned over and told him that it was the wrong exit for Baghdad. Neither the driver nor the man in the back said a word. A few minutes later the fat man piped up.

'This is a much shorter route into town. I am sure you need all the time you can get to make the most of your night out.'

We both thanked the gentleman and couldn't believe our luck that we had found such an understanding person.

Fifteen minutes later, I started to recognise the road we were on: we were back on the main road towards our camp. My heart sank as I realised that we had not even seen the face of the man sat behind us. As the car pulled up to the gates and a heavy feeling hung in my stomach, soldiers ran towards us and saluted the man in the back.

He was the Chief Officer of Al Rashid, the highest-ranking officer of the camp. The On-Call Captain came running over to the car and we were dragged out at gunpoint towards the prison cells. My friend and I spent the rest of our time in military service in a prison cell. We were given less to eat and only had the concrete cell floor to sleep on. It was tough to stay strong, both mentally and physically.

Finally, on 21st December 1968, we were called out of prison. They were going to expedite our graduation from the camp as medical lieutenants because of a military coup against the government. At the graduation ceremony, there was a military parade in front of the Minister of Defence. I was asked to lead the parade carrying the Iraqi flag. I never knew why I had been chosen but years later discovered that my Uncle, a high-ranking officer, had organised this honour.

I continued the rest of my military service and eventually finished in 1970, following two gruelling years. It was then that I decided to follow my dream and head to England to train in surgery.

LOVE AT FIRST SIGHT

I arrived in England just before Christmas 1970. I started my first job at New Cross Hospital in Wolverhampton as a Senior House Officer in Orthopaedics. After four years, in May 1975, I got my fellowship from the Royal College of Surgeons in Edinburgh with a distinction. From 1975 I was a Registrar in the Isle of Wight for two years, moved on to St. Mark's and then to St. Bartholomew's Hospital in London.

I eventually returned to the Isle of Wight in 1978 as a Locum Consultant. I had been pushed through the system rapidly and progressed from Senior House Officer level to become a Consultant Surgeon in a record number of years. I was advised by my Senior Consultants' colleagues not to return to Iraq because I would waste the status and academic achievement that I had worked for in England.

Whilst I was at New Cross Hospital I made many friends and knew everyone in the hospital; I had a great social life. I remember one day I was called by the Sister on Ward 8, the surgical ward, to see a patient. At the time it was customary that whenever a Doctor arrived on the ward, the on-duty Sister would allocate a chaperone nurse to visit the patient with them. This time Sister Schofield allocated a young pre-nursing cadet to me that I had never seen before.

It was love at first sight. She took my breath away. The nurse was the most naturally beautiful woman I had ever laid eyes on, yet she radiated a certain sense of innocence that I had never found in another woman. Her smile was simply infectious and it managed to light up any room she walked into.

She never uttered a word when we first met but showed me to the patient and stayed until I had finished the examination. It was one of the longest history taking sessions I had ever done because I wanted to keep her by my side for as long as I could. I don't know how I knew, but I knew I was in love with her. I had to see her again.

From then on Ward 8 became my favourite ward and I would find any excuse to go down there to catch a glimpse of her beauty. Unfortunately, I never saw her again. I, along with all the other Doctors, was very afraid of the senior Matron. I was even too scared to ask for the girl's full name. I went to every single surgical ward and even started going for breakfast, lunch and dinner in the main hospital restaurant, rather than eating with the other Doctors in the Doctor's lounge, in the simple hope that I would just see her one more time. She had completely vanished and I never found out her name or the nature of her placement.

One Friday afternoon, I was shopping in the Mander Centre in Wolverhampton. I spotted her through the window of Woolworths, I couldn't believe my luck so I tried to relax my nerves and approached her.

'Hello there,' I said.

She turned and looked at me, gave a big smile and returned my greeting, blushing deeply.

'What are you doing here Doctor?'

Suddenly, realising that this was my only opportunity to get to know her better, I began lying through my teeth.

'I am looking to buy something for my sister in Iraq and I'm useless at choosing things for women, I would really appreciate it if you could help me.'

The young nurse agreed instantly and I felt like it was fate. I invited her for a coffee in the shopping mall to tell her more about my sister and the fake present that she could help me decide to buy. We sat in the café and introduced ourselves.

Her name was Mary. Her Father was an Irishman and her Mother English. She had one younger brother and was originally from Ireland, County Donegal. She had moved to the West Midlands when she was five years-old. I remember at that moment, whilst she was talking, my eyes were fixated on her lips yet I couldn't concentrate on the words coming out of them as questions were darting around my brain. How would I keep her talking? When would I see her again? Is she currently in a relationship? Thankfully, as we carried on talking, I discovered that she wasn't yet spoken for.

We left the café and went shopping for my sister. When we finished I thanked her for all her help and offered to give her a lift home in my car. She refused and said that she preferred to get the bus. I did somehow manage to get her phone number, and that was the start of our relationship.

THE DRIVE TO IRAQ

After a couple of years of being together, I suggested to Mary that she should visit Iraq so that she could make up her mind about where she wanted to live in the long-term. I tried to explain the differences in culture and religion, but knew that she couldn't get a true picture without actually visiting the country.

At the time I was unable to go back home, so Mary decided to visit Iraq alone and stay with my family. Something I can't imagine a lot of women being willing to do, this was just another indication of how brilliant the woman I had found was. I called my parents and my brothers and told them that she was coming over, and that I wanted them to show her our everyday lives. I told them not to act any differently whilst she was there. It was important for her to see both the good and the bad sides of living in Iraq.

Mary went over and spent a month with my family, visiting both the rundown slums and the most beautiful places in Babylon. It went exactly as I had hoped. She met all of my family, friends and neighbours and settled in better than expected. She loved and was loved by all the people around her. Mary even went to visit the religious holy places of Kabala and Najef. When she showed me the photos, I remember thinking how beautiful she managed to look in the Arabic *Abaya*; the long black cover warn by women in some Arab countries, which she had to wear to visit the holy places.

My parents told me that Mary was more Arabic than any other Arabic girl as she seemed to love every aspect of the culture; from the food to the clothes to the large family gatherings. I remember them telling me that they felt so close to her that they wanted her to stay in Iraq.

We got married on 12th September 1975 and a year later we had our first child, Marwan; our beautiful baby boy. We moved to the Isle of Wight and it was there that we stayed up one night discussing our life plans. We decided that we would go back to Iraq and that we would go by car.

A couple of years before, the Iraqi government had issued regulations to tempt academics working abroad, mainly Doctors and Engineers, to come back to Iraq to avoid what is known as a 'brain drain' on the economy. The Iraqi Embassy in London sent me a letter notifying me that if I decided to go back to Iraq, I would be entitled to a brand new tax-free car and house, a free piece of land and fully-paid travel expenses for myself and my family. At that time, tax on imported cars in Iraq was 300% and on furniture it was 200%, so their offer was a massive temptation.

Many people returned to Iraq with these incentives. The type of car you could take back with you was restricted to three models: a Peugeot, a Volvo or a Fiat. The Government did not allow the public to drive cars such as Mercedes, BMW or Jaguar as these were their cars of choice and nobody was to be confused as a member of the government. You were also not allowed a black or beige car as black vehicles represented the President's vehicles and beige cars represented the military. They also ordered that no car had tinted glass on the windows or have a radio aerial at the back. In fact, Iraqis were not even allowed sunscreens on the car to shield themselves from the scorching sun.

At the time that they issued this offer I had been working in Wales, so I travelled to London to meet the Cultural Attaché. I told him that I thought the incentives were good and I was willing to go back eventually, but I felt that I needed more time to gain experience as an independent Consultant. I asked for permission to stay in the UK for two more years before taking up the generous offer. As I expected, he outright refused; the Iraqi government had clearly stated that you had to be back in Iraq before 1st January 1977, otherwise you would lose all rights to be considered under this scheme. I hadn't been ready to return at that point, and gaining more experience to become a better Surgeon was far more important than material goods, so I decided to stay in the UK and I didn't take up their offer.

Now that we had decided that we were going back to Iraq, I contacted the Embassy again to see if there was any chance of me being entitled to the incentives that they had previously offered. I knew it was a lost cause, but that there was no harm in trying.

I also wanted to notify the Embassy that I would be returning to Iraq with an English wife. At the time government rules stated that an Iraqi married to a foreign wife could not work in a government hospital and I wanted to find a loophole. Finding that the Embassy had no real power, I decided to write a personal letter to the President at the time, Ahmed Hassan Al Baker. I sent a copy of the letter to his Vice President, Saddam Hussein.

In the letter, I explained my situation and the reasons for not taking up the incentives when they were originally offered. I mentioned that I had married an English woman and that I hoped when I returned we would both be welcomed in Iraq. Soon after I wrote the letter I bought a brand new beige Volvo fitted with sunscreens in the back as I felt it was essential to protect Mary and Marwan from the burning sun along the way. It was the only available duty-free car with middle-eastern specification at the Volvo dealership in London. I didn't think about the dangers of the Iraqi regulations, hoping that I would not get pulled up for it.

We set off on our drive to Iraq on my birthday, 21st September 1978. All my friends and family warned us about the risks and the problems of driving through Turkey. We were told that although the Turkish were normally appear very friendly, it was common for many tourists driving through the country to be victims of corruption and robbery. Ignoring the dangers and seeking adventure, I began the long drive with my two year old son and Mary, who was three months pregnant.

The drive through Europe was lovely. We stopped for a few nights along the way in both Western and Eastern European countries. We didn't have any problems until we crossed into Turkey on 2nd October 1978; an experience that we will never forget. We drove straight to Istanbul, which was our first stop. Our car was loaded with a lot of expensive goods: cameras, videos, computers, expensive surgical equipment and presents for my family such as watches and fur coats. I didn't want to ship them to Iraq with the rest of our belongings because I didn't trust that they would ever get there.

When we crossed the border into Turkey, we were told about a four star hotel and made our way there. As it was difficult to empty the car for one night at a hotel, we decided that it was much better to get a respectable hotel where the car might be safely locked in their car park.

When we arrived at the hotel we found that it was perfect; it had a huge private car park, a grand entrance and beautiful en-suite rooms. Our room was wonderful; we had a private staircase from our balcony leading down to the beach. I completed the check-in documents and took Mary and Marwan to the room. I left her to settle and unpack our suitcases and went down to the reception desk to ask about the restaurant and other facilities at the hotel.

At the hotel reception a man wearing a red jacket, black trousers and a gold badge with 'Saleem' written on it was very polite and answered all my queries. He asked me if the UK-registered Volvo was mine and he said that the car seemed to be loaded with boxes that seemed quite valuable. He told me that it was unsafe to leave it unattended and suggested that I either empty our belongings into the room or if I wished, I could park it in a special place just outside the main entrance to the hotel where he would keep an eye on it. He said it would only cost £50 for the night but that I would need to pay in advance. I agreed to pay for the one night and brought the car round to park it where he had directed me. I noted that the other places beside me were reserved for the Director of the hotel and other staff, but he assured me that it was fine for me to park there.

I returned to the room and told Mary about the secure arrangements of the car and suggested that we should stay three nights as it seemed like a nice place to relax. We changed into our clothes for dinner and went downstairs to change some money for the evening. Saleem wasn't behind the desk but instead there was another employee in the exact same uniform. I changed some money and before I left, he asked me if the Volvo with the UK registration plate was mine. He said that it was parked illegally and I had to move it otherwise I would be fined. I explained the agreement that I had made with Saleem less than an hour ago and that I had already paid money up front to park it securely in that spot. The man behind the desk appeared confused.

'Nobody that works here is called Saleem, Sir, and I have not left reception for the last two hours, you must be mistaken.'

We got into a heated debate and a German gentleman who had apparently overhead the discussion headed towards me. He quickly explained how he had just paid 200 deutschmarks to be able to park his car right next to my Volvo and that the hotel was also now denying the existence of Saleem.

Together we insisted on speaking to the hotel manager, who in return only supported the man behind the reception desk and denied that there was ever any employee by that name or description. He asked us both to move our cars before they imposed a heavy fine on us. I moved it back to the guest space and after our rushed dinner, which was interrupted by my frequent inspections of the car, Mary and Marwan went to the room and I went to sleep in the car.

As I was sitting behind the wheel trying to think about the best way to deal with this problem, I noticed Saleem leave the hotel at the end of his shift wearing his uniform. He disappeared in an Anadol; a small white locally made car. I knew we had to leave Istanbul at first light.

At 5am the following morning, we left the hotel without breakfast. From Istanbul, we wished to go straight to Iraq but it was impossible to do as Turkey is a vast country and I had a pregnant wife and a two year-old son with me. So, we drove to Ankara, which was the next big city on our route. We drove all that day and through the night, not wanting to stop at any other point along the way. We decided that the safest thing to do was to sleep in the daytime only and drive through the night. So when we arrived at our hotel in Ankara, Mary and Marwan went into the hotel to have a nap and I stayed in the car to protect it and all of our goods. When night fell, we carried on our drive through Diyarbakir and finally Silopi. Silopi is the official passport checkpoint separated from Iraqi soil only by a short fifty-metre bridge.

At Silopi I left Mary and Marwan in the car and went to show our passports to Border Control. I was directed to the room of the police officer who dealt with the exit visas from Turkey. I walked into the room and a very friendly First Lieutenant sat behind a desk piled full of passports. I stood patiently in the queue and when it was my turn I approached the desk and handed him our passports. He put them in the

The Hanging Gardens of Babylon

pile with the rest of the passports, handed me a piece of paper and told me that I had to fill it out to be able to pay for the exit.

I quickly entered my details onto the form and returned to his room. Another police officer was sitting in his place; I explained that I had filled out all the paperwork and had returned to pick up our passports. The Captain looked at me in confusion. He told me that nobody had to pay an exit fee and that the form was nothing to do with me leaving the country. At this point I was more than ready to leave and simply wanted our passports safely back in my hand.

He opened the drawers of the desk and searched the pile of passports but ours were nowhere to be found. He asked me if I was sure I had given the previous police officer our passports and tried to convince me that I was tired and confused from all the travelling. Seeing the reaction on my face, he clearly felt sorry for me and told me that his colleague had only gone home and would be back early in the morning.

I began to panic. What would we do in this small village scattered with muddy huts and with my wife and baby son in the car? There were no hotels for miles and there was no way that we could tolerate staying out in the sweltering heat for another sixteen hours. The only thing separating me and Iraqi soil was a very small bridge; I could actually see the Iraqis ahead of me at Ibrahim Al-Khalil. I wished I could have shouted to them for help.

I returned to the car in panic, wondering how I would be able to keep Mary calm. Once I had told her the news, she broke down in tears. The events of the last few days had taken their toll and this was the last thing we needed. Mary was extremely upset and agreed that there was no way we could wait in the car until morning following our long journey from Ankara.

We felt really low and desperate; we just wanted to get into Iraq. A young man was watching from a distance. He began to approach the car, dressed casually in a short sleeved t-shirt and trousers he looked quite respectable.

'Hi,' he said, 'why is the Madam crying and upset?'

I explained everything to him.

'Don't worry sir, don't worry at all,' he said with confidence. 'I know the Lieutenant and he is a very nice person. I also know where he lives and can get your passports back to you.'

I could have kissed his hand. Before I even took a breath to thank him for his act of kindness, he continued, 'It will cost you $200.'

I didn't care how much money it would cost to get us home, I would have paid anything at that moment in time just to cross the border. I agreed immediately, but knowing how things seemed to work in this town, I told him that I would give him $50 now and the rest when we had our passports in hand.

He disappeared with the $50 and within the longest hour of our lives, returned with our passports. Now, I was only fifty metres away from Iraq, the home that I had left eight years before. I got back into the car; Mary was over the moon and we were ready to leave.

As I started the engine and looked in my rear view mirror, I realised that I had been closed in by two local cars. There was absolutely no way that I could manoeuvre the Volvo out of the space that we were in. Luckily the driver of the vehicle in front was sitting in his car so I got out and asked him to move slightly forwards. He told me that his car had broken down and that he didn't have any money to call out a mechanic to repair it. I couldn't believe what I was hearing, but quickly knew that I would have to play this game yet again in order to get anywhere. He told me that it would cost $100 to move the car a few metres forward, but I only had $50 left on me.

'Move the car forward and when I reach the bridge I will give you $50,' I promised him, desperate to leave.

He began to think about my offer, but I interrupted by telling him calmly that the alternative would involve me smashing into the back of his car and pushing it forwards myself. He realised that I was very serious and meant what I said so he moved his car forward.

'Now walk in front of me to the bridge,' I told him. 'I don't want any more problems, and then I will give you the money.'

He did exactly as I said and I handed him the money, only once I knew very well that there was only the barrier to be lifted and I could go across to my country.

When I drove into Iraq across the border to Ibrahim Al-Khalil Passport Centre a mixture of emotions stole over me. I was stepping onto Iraqi soil for the first time in eight years. I was about to meet my people again, the Iraqis whom I loved and respected highly. I had left my country with a big smile on my face and returned to it with tears in my eyes.

The welcome we received from the officers in Passport Control was exactly what I expected. I was so proud that this was my 'home sweet home'. The moment we walked in, they pulled out a chair for Mary and put a cushion on the seat to protect her from the harsh metal. They poured her a mint tea and got her and Marwan a glass of cold water; the Iraqi way of hospitality to foreigners. We then drove straight to Mosul where we spent the night. The following day we drove south to Baghdad where we stopped for dinner before continuing on our journey to Babylon; my hometown.

The reunion with my family was very emotional and we didn't sleep at all that night. All my family were gathered around us and a great feeling of excitement was in the air. Everyone pressed in to see the new additions to the family; Mary and Marwan. We were spoiled to death. We stayed at my father's house: a massive property built on 7,000m^2 with seven bedrooms in the main house and three other annexe houses connected to the main one through long, secure glass corridors. Each one of the small houses had three bedrooms, a kitchen, two bathrooms and a small garden. The house was surrounded by a beautiful orchard and had a small swimming pool to the front. This was my paradise.

LIFE BACK IN IRAQ

After a few days rest in Babylon, I went to Baghdad with all the official papers I needed to get an appointment with the Ministry of Health. On arrival at the Ministry I was given a very warm welcome and directed to the Managing Director's office, the official who was in charge of handling my request. After the usual chat and a cup of tea he asked me where I wanted to work in Iraq.

'In Babylon please,' I told him. 'I would like to be near my family and with my wife being foreign she may settle better with my family around.'

He told me that it was impossible. Babylon had been closed for any further medical appointments by the Minister of Health, as it was so popular and in demand by returning medical staff. He told me that I could choose any city in Iraq including Basra, which was also famous for teaching hospitals and medical schools. I politely insisted that Babylon was my only choice because of Mary. He went into the Minister's office and within five minutes he came back and told me that the Minister of Health wanted to see me.

That was the first time that I met with the Minister of Health, Dr Riad Ibrahim, a gynaecologist, who had been a few years senior to me at the same medical school. He was from a very well known and highly respected family and had a very wealthy father. He was renowned for his exceptional manners and ethics in all conduct. The Minister was waiting for me at the door of his office. He didn't sit behind the desk after he welcomed me with a handshake, but sat in front of me on the leather sofa as though we were old friends.

'Well, Ismaiel,' he said. 'We have received correspondence from the President's Office in response to a letter that you wrote to them. They have asked to be informed upon your arrival in Iraq and your making contact with us. Therefore, I cannot do anything without receiving further instructions from the President or the Vice President.'

Without waiting for me to respond he reached for his telephone and spoke to somebody, telling them that Dr Ismaiel Bhayah was back from England and sitting in front of him. He put the telephone down and turned to me with a smile on his face.

'You have to go to the Ministry of Education, 9th Floor, to see Mr Almasi, who has all the communication and correspondence regarding your letters to the President.'

I got straight into my car and drove to the Ministry of Education in Al Jadderia. At reception a message had been left under my name saying that I was to be shown immediately to the 9th floor. I must admit the mysterious orders unnerved me quite a bit, but having grown up with the Iraqi way of life I automatically complied without hesitation.

The receptionist jumped out of her seat and led me to the 9th floor where Mr Almasi was waiting for me.

'Dr Ismaiel, we have been really looking forward to meeting you Sir,' he said. 'Welcome home and a big welcome to your wife and family.'

He then invited me to walk with him back to his office. It was an elegant office, made up of mahogany wood, leather furniture and many beautiful ornaments. He had one single file in front of him on the desk, entitled 'Dr Ismaiel Bhayah - Correspondence with His Excellency the President'.

After an initial chat and friendly exchange of views about England and Iraq, and the value of returning home, he got down to business. He opened the file in front of him and read to me what the President had commented as a footnote on my original letter. The President had written in red: 'Inform us on his arrival to the country and let us know his needs.' Underneath was the signature of the President, Ahmed Hassan Al-Baker. A copy of my letter to the Vice President had also been filed in the same folder and there was a comment on it by Saddam's personal secretary to the same effect: 'Inform us on his arrival, his demands are to be granted'. This was signed by the personal secretary to Saddam Hussein.

Mr Almasi took a blank piece of paper and started writing a draft letter, to be typed later. It was addressed to the President and Vice President's office.

'What shall we request from them?'

Without giving me a chance to respond he started the usual protocol letter and added that I wished to be appointed in Babylon, to be exempt from the law of marriage to non-Arabic wives, and to be allowed to keep my car and buy my house furniture free of tax.

He looked up at me.

'Is that all?' he asked.

'Yes, that is more than enough' I replied.

'That is nothing Dr Ismaiel, we are writing to the men who run our country,' and then he continued writing whilst he was talking out loud, 'he would also like to have a large piece of land in Babylon, have his journey by car from England fully paid for, have the fine that was taken from him when he left the country to be repaid and be supplied with a telephone line in both his home and his clinic'.

At that time you could wait up to four years to have a telephone line installed in your house. He concluded the letter by saying that if the President's office wanted to add anything as a welcome gift, it would be most welcomed.

I thought the letter had asked for too much, but he insisted that they were acceptable and reasonable things to ask for. I wasn't expecting any of the above; all I had wanted was to be exempt from the law of marrying a foreign wife. If they hadn't exempted me, I would have been forbidden from working in a government hospital and my children would not have been able to go to school in Iraq. I shook hands with Mr Almasi and thanked him for all his help.

I then went back home to tell Mary about the unbelievable story on my first working day back in Iraq. Five days later the Minister of Health rang me personally.

'Congratulations, Doctor,' he said. 'All of your requests have been granted and you will be appointed in Babylon. Also, the President's office has sent a copy of the Presidential Order to all offices that you might need to deal with to facilitate and expedite the routine bureaucracy.'

He went on to tell me that the Presidential Declaration not only exempt me from the law of marriage to foreign wives, but that the President had also granted Mary the right to work in Iraq if she so wished. This was unheard of in Iraq.

It was a great start to my life back home: I was appointed at Babylon Surgical Hospital, given a large piece of land to build a house and within a week the Office of Telecommunications contacted me to install two telephone lines, one in my house and one in my private clinic. This was all published in the official government newspaper *Al-Wakae'al Iraqia*, where all government declarations were published.

The fact that I was from a *Sayed* family helped me to quickly establish a superb surgical practice. I became one of the most well known figures in Surgery. The people from Babylon were mainly Sheas, and great believers in Saint Ali, the son-in-law of Prophet Mohammed. Therefore they always considered us as a holy family.

People would greet us by bowing their head and kissing our hands. Even when my children were with me older men and women insisted on kissing their hands as a blessing. Patients started coming from all over the country to see me, I even had patients travel from Kuwait and Qatar. My private practice was booming and life was going well. That was until 16th March 1979.

AN EARLY GOODBYE

I vividly remember 14th March 1979 as a nice, warm spring day. We were still living in my Father's house and we had arranged a big garden party with family and friends. The kids had decided to paddle in the pool at the front of the house. Marwan my son had joined in with his cousins, enjoying splashing around and playing in the water. I was with him the whole time and it was a fun day for all the family. Later, we had an open air barbeque followed by cakes and drinks.

The following day, I went to the hospital for my theatre list. At about 11 a.m. whilst I was mid-operation on a man, Mary rang to say that Marwan was not well. He had woken up with vomiting and diarrhoea. I knew that Mary wouldn't call me at work if she didn't feel that he was seriously ill. I left theatre as soon as I had finished the operation and on my way home I called in to see one of my paediatrician colleagues to take his advice about Marwan's symptoms.

The paediatrician, out of courtesy and friendship, followed me home to see my son. After listening to Mary's account of his symptoms, he thoroughly examined Marwan and assured us that there was nothing seriously wrong with him. He thought that his symptoms were related to excessive playing

The Hanging Gardens of Babylon

and eating in the hot sun at the garden party, in a climate to which he hadn't yet acclimatised.

After the Doctor left, I stayed with Mary and Marwan for the rest of the afternoon but a few hours later Marwan's condition deteriorated rapidly. I contacted my friend again to express my concern about his illness and he came round immediately with another paediatrician to examine him at home. This time they decided to give him some oral antibiotics and told us to encourage him to drink plenty of fluids.

By 7 pm Marwan's fever was so high, and he was complaining continuously, that I decided to take him to see a very senior paediatrician in Baghdad. The paediatrician was also very reassuring and advised us to continue giving him plenty of oral fluids and paracetamol. He was very confident that there was nothing serious and he advised us to go back to Babylon to allow him to rest, promising to call us the following morning to check on his progress.

We arrived back in Babylon at around 10.30pm. Marwan, at that stage, had begun vomiting again and had become extremely drowsy. I contacted the two consultants in Babylon who had already seen him that morning; we were very worried that there was something seriously wrong with our son. The two Doctors examined him again and decided to give him intravenous fluid and intravenous antibiotics. They left our house after midnight, with another promise to check on him in the morning.

I put Marwan on my lap and Mary sat beside me. I must have dozed off with him on my lap, but Mary did not close her eyes once that night, watching us both. Suddenly I was woken up by Mary shouting, 'Marwan's not well. I think he's fading'. I opened my eyes and looked down at him. His skin was blue and he had started convulsing, with froth in his mouth. Frightened, Mary kept shouting that he was going. I picked him up, jumped into my car and drove to the Paediatric Hospital in Babylon that was less than half a mile away from our house.

I rushed him into the Resuscitation Room. There was absolutely nothing in the room to resuscitate him with. No suction pump, no oxygen, nothing at all. There was not one Doctor or nurse around. I picked up a rubber tube that I found in the corner of the room, placed it in his mouth and started to suck out his airways with my mouth. I then began CPR (Cardio Pulmonary Resuscitation) whilst Mary tried to give him the kiss of life. There was no response to all that we were doing. Marwan did not open his eyes again. That was the last moment that we were to spend with our son alive.

Doctors and nurses began to turn up at the hospital because they had heard that I was there. They were trying to drag Mary and me away from his small, lifeless body. They tried to take him away from me but I hugged him to my chest, hoping that something miraculous would happen and he would open his eyes or speak to us. By that time there was a massive crowd around Mary and me. My brothers arrived at the hospital. They took Marwan's body from me and escorted Mary and me to the car to take us back to the house. We left Marwan behind in the Resuscitation Room in the hands of strangers.

To walk into the house at that time was the worst psychological trauma I have ever experienced. Toys, nappies and baby clothes were strewn across the house. All were now nothing but memories of our son. It is difficult to express in words, the feeling that we had that day: the feeling of parents who had walked out of the house with a two year-old son and returned home without him.

It was midnight and I didn't want Marwan to be alone with strangers. I experienced an irrational feeling that he may feel lonely during the night, that he would be scared and looking for us. This feeling was so compelling that I got back into my car and drove to the hospital. I saw my brother Ahmed at the hospital, who reassured me that he would spend the whole night with Marwan and would not leave him alone. That didn't matter; I told him I would stay through the night in case Marwan wanted me.

After he was buried, I visited Marwan's grave daily. At night, I would go there and sit beside him to tell him bedtime stories. On his birthday, I would buy him toys and take them to him. I felt better when I was physically closer to him, as though he knew I was there and hadn't forgotten him.

I also made sure that he was not alone in his grave; he was buried next to my grandparents whom I loved a lot, because I wanted him to lay next to somebody that I trusted to look after him. Despite the hardships in life that my Father had warned us about, and the gruelling years of military service, neither had prepared me to deal with this. If it were not for Mary being so emotionally and mentally strong I would not have had the strength to continue living.

I felt in debt to the Minister of Health. As soon as he heard the news, he got into his car and came to see us with his condolences. He gave us an unqualified offer to do what we wanted, to leave Iraq for a holiday or even for good. His support helped us to cope with our loss. We went to England for a few weeks in order to clear our minds and get away from the memories of our son.

After five weeks in England, we decided that Iraq was home and that we would return with our two month-old daughter May, to attempt to piece our lives back together. People said that time would heal the wounds but it never did.

WAR

After our break in the UK, we returned to Iraq in May 1979. We moved out of my Father's house and rented our own, hoping to get away from the surroundings that reminded us of Marwan. We made a conscious effort to try and live a normal life, and focused our attention on May and each other.

Iraq was flourishing at the time with stable social conditions and these conditions made us think that we had made the right decision to come back. My work at the government hospital continued to make me feel content through helping the community and my private practice was extremely successful. I was becoming very highly respected and well known as a Doctor. Those around us supported us in every aspect of our lives. The income from my private practice was escalating rapidly and patients would bring me expensive gifts as a token of appreciation that I had made time to see them.

In the summer of 1979 Saddam took over as President of Iraq from President Ahmed Hassan Al-Baker, who was forced to resign with what was announced as 'health problems'. Saddam brought massive improvements to the infrastructure of Iraq and the standard of living for all. However, from the outset Saddam made it clear that he would not tolerate disloyal Iraqis.

If you could avoid getting involved in any political discussions or activities associated with his regime, you could guarantee yourself a fairly comfortable and decent living. In the first twelve months of Saddam's leadership, the standard of living improved so dramatically that there was no restriction in travelling abroad. Even those people on limited incomes managed for the very first time to afford to travel to Eastern and Western Europe. Suddenly there were new hospitals, new roads, new hotels, clean water and electricity to all parts of Iraq including the most remote villages. The Iraqi dinar had never been so strong.

One hot evening at the end of September 1980, it was announced on the radio and television that the Iraqi army had spun into conflict with Iran. The Iraqis attacked Iranian soldiers on Iranian land to push them back from invading Iraq. An hour later, the whole of Iraq descended into darkness. An air siren warned of an attack on Iraqi cities, but fortunately nothing happened. The war had officially begun and we were led to believe it would be a quick Iraqi victory with aid from the UN. We couldn't have been more wrong. We were blissfully unaware of the brutal eight year war that lay ahead of us.

The next day at work, the Director of the hospital called an emergency meeting. He had brought with him representatives from both the Ba'ath Party and the Security Department, who were known as Al-Amin. We were told that there had been heavy fighting on the front and that there were already hundreds of injured soldiers.

They were looking for volunteers to go to the frontline hospitals. It was at that very moment that the concept of war became a hard reality. This is the first taste of war my generation had experienced. Overnight we had become involved in vicious conflict with our neighbours, and now we were being asked to physically contribute. What this really meant, and where we would be going and how close to the fighting we were going to get, nobody dared to ask. In the meeting it was clear that they were only looking for general surgeons, orthopaedic surgeons and anaesthetists at this stage.

I knew from experience that the word 'voluntary' was nothing more than a test of your loyalty, rather than an actual option. I also knew that eventually we would all have to go to the frontline and there was no use in tarnishing my name by not demonstrating my loyalty.

I was not a member of the Ba'ath Party and never registered with them, yet as I raised my hand I noticed that I was first in the room to volunteer. As soon as I had declared my willingness to go, everybody seemed surprised, in particular from the Ba'ath Party and Al-Amin representatives, who within minutes had reported the results of the meeting to their Headquarters. The expression on their faces was a mixture of respect and admiration.

The others slowly raised their hands one by one. Eventually, under the piercing eyes of Al-Amin, every Doctor in the room had volunteered to go to the war front. We asked when and how we were going to deliver our services.

The Ba'ath Party representative answered: 'In a rota, two general surgeons, one orthopaedic surgeon and one anaesthetist with all theatre staff will constitute a team. Each will have a rota and take turns to go to the frontline'.

Before leaving he turned to me and said, 'I am, on behalf of the Ba'ath Party, grateful for your support and your attitude. We all know that you have just arrived from England and that you have recently lost your son and that this will involve you leaving your British wife behind. Your immediate response has been noted and reported to our Headquarters. Thank you once again.'

As the officials began leaving the room, one of them turned to our Director and said, 'By the way, the first Doctor has to be at the frontline tomorrow morning'.

Immediately our Director asked us to team ourselves into four groups, each consisting of two general surgeons, one orthopaedic surgeon and one anaesthetist. He left us to decide between us which Doctor would go first tomorrow. The most senior surgeon in the room was also a member of the Ba'ath Party and was actually in charge of the Ba'ath Party organisation in our hospital. He suggested that we pull names out of a hat. The way I saw it, was that we had to go whether we were first or last it didn't make a difference. I didn't want to be involved in these childish games so I turned to him and said, 'You pull names out of a hat, I will go first.'

Two hours later I was contacted by the Ba'ath Party Headquarters and invited to meet the head of the Ba'ath Party in Babylon. The news had reached them that not only had I volunteered first but that I had also chosen to go to the frontline tomorrow.

Turning down such an invitation was definitely not an option. When I arrived at the Party Headquarters I was well received and treated with respect. The soldiers were saluting me as if I was a military officer. They took me straight into the office, which was full of other high ranking military officers, and the Mayor of Babylon.

The Mayor was Saddam's brother-in-law. The Head of the Party was at the end of a room sitting behind a large desk. I was warmly welcomed by all of them, especially the Mayor, who reminded me that we had actually met in *Al-Mahaweel;* the military camp at which I was a Medical Lieutenant and Acting Commander in Charge of the Military Hospital before I went to England. He reminded the others of my contribution to improve the health service in the camp. I could not remember doing anything special, but thanked him for his kind praise.

That meeting was nothing more than a welcome and social chat about England, my studies and training. Before I left, they insisted that I was to give Mary their telephone number and that she was to ring them if she ever needed anything. The Mayor of Babylon even offered to send somebody to do her daily shopping for her. He then assured me that my house would be closely guarded by soldiers to comfort me that in my absence Mary was not to fear anything whilst she was on her own in the house with our little girl.

These reassurances and special attention reinforced my initial thoughts that volunteering from the start was a smart move.

THE FRONTIER HOSPITALS

Within the first year the war had escalated to a stage where anybody who went near the frontier risked being killed or taken as a prisoner of war by the Iranians. Stories of people disappearing had filled nearby towns and cities with fear. Both sides had realised that there was no easy way to end the fighting. The political world, especially America and England, were thoroughly enjoying the situation and were viciously fuelling the war machine to keep it active. Their two worst enemies, Iran and Iraq, were fighting each other, exhausting their reserves, men and power and driving their oil resources to the West.

The American and European weapons markets were thriving, both were competing for arms sales to both sides. It felt like the rest of the world was turning a cold shoulder to us, and some of them even contributing to our misery, while our country suffered in silence. The war killed the innocent in droves and degraded the quality of our lives on a daily basis.

I will never forget the famous words of American Foreign Secretary, Henry Kissinger: 'This is the only war in history for which we hope there shall be no winner. Both sides will be losers in the end'. In fact, it was in America's hands to decide who would win or lose, depending on where they judged their own interests to lie. They realised that their interests lay in both sides losing, with the war destroying our lives and killing thousands. They certainly got what they wished for.

There were three main towns at a short distance from the frontier with Iran. From north to south there was Mandali, about six kilometres away from Iran, Al-Omara, about twenty-five kilometres away, and Basra, which was more or less sat at the boundary with Iran. Standing on the bank of the river that divided the two countries, Iraqi's and Iranian's could hear the other side shouting at them from the opposite bank.

The schedule allowed for each team to go to one of the above locations for two weeks at a time, during which we would be resident at the local hospital. We would do an on-call rota on an eight hour basis. In reality, of course, the length of your shift could never be dictated, as injured soldiers could turn up at any time.

Sometimes, when there was heavy fighting, the evacuation of casualties was immense and people were carried out by cars, aeroplanes, helicopters and buses that had been transformed into makeshift ambulances. The number of casualties and the type of injuries we would see varied greatly. During heavy attacks we would receive thousands of patients at the hospital door and we had to be very well-organised in order to deal with the most serious casualties first. We would transfer some of the less serious cases out to the main hospital inland to ease the crowds of people we had to deal with.

With the presence of other teams like ours from all over the country there were at least ten to fifteen general surgeons on-call in any one shift. There were other specialist surgeons supporting us: neurosurgeons, thoracic surgeons and maxillofacial surgeons. Generally, those cases that had ear, nose and throat injuries or eye damage could always be transferred to the inland hospital.

The facilities for treatment were first-class and the availability of surgical equipment, suture material, drains, theatre furniture, chest tubes, intravenous fluid replacement and blood were not only available in abundance but they were probably the best in the world. We had no financial difficulties or restrictions placed on us. When we asked for something we got it. All the transport for medical equipment was done by air.

The only restricting factor was the theatre space. Although they had converted ordinary rooms in the hospital into theatres, they were not very effective due to their location. Due to the lack of space, we would sometimes operate on any table we could find, such as a dining table, using a mobile light projector simply because the priority was to save a life, not to use the right equipment.

Patients, regardless of how major their operation was, would be transferred to their local hospital inland within twenty-four hours. My team did not have one single loss of life in transport or death mid-operation. It was when I was serving at the frontline that I first realised the influence that Saddam had at every level of every department in the country – he may have caused a much higher proportion of deaths but, when it was needed for his people, he saved lives through an incomparable medical service.

The Hanging Gardens of Babylon

On one occasion in 1982, following fighting on the frontline, my list of patients needing abdominal surgery was totalling thirty at a time. Evacuations of injured soldiers would continue to pour in and I had to operate quickly and safely. I went to the Operating Theatre and grabbed two junior Doctors to help me with a long waiting list. I asked them to bring with them two mobile stretchers and place them either side of the main operating table. I brought in three patients and laid them side by side, asking the only anaesthetist available to give them anaesthesia, assisted and supported by two anaesthetic assistants.

The three patients were anaesthetised in one go and I delegated the cases according to the seriousness of the case to the junior Doctors. I asked each of them to open the abdomen and to shout out their findings; that way I could guide them through what to do and help anyone that was struggling. I operated on the most difficult and complicated case of the three, whilst watching over the two juniors either side of me.

When the trainee opened an abdomen and it was something they could deal with I would give them the necessary instructions. If there was an organ or an injury that they couldn't deal with, I would swap places with them, deal with the life-threatening situation – such as heavy bleeding from a spleen, liver or kidney – stabilise the patient and then ask the trainee to tidy up and close the abdomen. My colleague general surgeons, who had similar casualty lists, began to follow the same procedure.

The Hospital Director heard what I was doing and came down to theatre to ask staff about how the process was going.

They told him that I was working at a rapid pace and that each of the patients was safe and well.

To keep my blood sugar stable, and to maintain my concentration, the theatre nurses would put sweets and chocolate in my mouth whilst I operated, and give me water through a straw to keep me hydrated. I didn't stop operating for hours. The patients would come in and out of the room on stretchers as though on a conveyor belt. The Director, a military pharmacist, opened the theatre door and asked me to stop for a break but I insisted on finishing another round of patients.

'Dr Ismaiel, this is not a request, it is a military order. You have to stop and leave the theatre.'

I tidied up the cases I was working on and left the theatre immediately. I came out into the break area where fifteen of my colleagues were drinking tea and coffee on their break. When I sat down the Hospital Director asked me if I was hungry and sent for an order or food and drink to be delivered to me.

He looked at me in a friendly way and said, 'Are you aware Dr Ismaiel of the time you have just spent in theatre?'

I didn't have a watch on and didn't think that I could have worked beyond my eight hour shift. I had been operating for twenty hours straight.

Unfazed I responded; 'Do you know that our problem here isn't the staff or the equipment. We have a lot of surgeons and anaesthetists sat around doing nothing. The problem is the theatre space to treat all the injured patients safely and effectively. To avoid what we are doing today, to get through my share of injured soldiers, I suggest that we need a suite of eight to ten theatres, which can be designed in a polygonal shape. The centre should be a scrub up area, the outermost part for the anaesthetic rooms and in between should be the theatres. If we had such a structure, the surgeons and anaesthetists would be able to communicate easily and safely in difficult situations and share experiences and opinions. It would effectively turn all of the operating theatre suites into a connected chain of rooms.'

At that time in Iraq, a Korean company had introduced a new building structure using ready-made walls that could lock with each other in a jigsaw fashion. I suggested that we use this structure; the water and electricity supplies were already incorporated in these walls according to the designers. This meant that apart from a solid concrete base required for any building, erection of the walls and the ceiling would take no time at all.

The Director listened with interest, but did not say anything. I went to my room for some rest so I was prepared for work the following day. At 6 a.m. I was woken up to be told that I was needed urgently in the Director's office. I shaved, got dressed quickly and went downstairs to see him. In his room there was a captain in military uniform pacing back and forth as though in a rush.

'Dr Ismaiel,' the Director said, 'your idea about theatre layout has been passed through the system and has reached Military Headquarters in Baghdad. They are going to fly you there to discuss your plan for the theatre space.'

He pointed at the Captain pacing the room and said, 'Captain Mohammed will be flying you to Baghdad. The helicopter is waiting for you in the hospital garden. You should be there in about two hours.'

At 9.30am, I was in Baghdad, sitting in a big conference room full of military officers at the Ministry of Defence. They asked me to sketch my idea on paper and to explain to them the practicalities from a surgical point of view. I told them that I thought it was the quickest, most cost-effective and space-saving solution to the problem of inadequate space and widely-scattered operating theatres. I also suggested that it could be done with the readymade cavity walls from the Korean company, explaining the time and cost implications. I was asked a few questions about the minimum size required for a comfortable operating theatre, the number of staff that would normally be circulating around, and other technical surgical matters like the flow from the scrub up room to theatre and how the patient would be mobilised in and out of the room.

That afternoon I was flown back to Al-Omara for my night shift. Exactly fourteen days later, the polygonal theatre complex had been finished.

It not only indicated an impressive and successful system which was desperately needed in a time of war, but also the watchful eye that Saddam had over every Iraqi person in society. Such control allowed him to use every resource his people had, as well as to quash those that showed opposition.

THE HARSH REALITY OF WAR

I witnessed unbelievable casualties during the eight-year war. I saw things no person should ever have to see. Gore beyond human comprehension. Nobody had taught us about the type of casualties we were going to encounter and no textbook had ever been written about these injuries. Twisted, mangled bodies encased the same poor souls that set out to help their country, and now they were in need of a degree of help that was difficult to provide. The casualties I dealt with were the most disturbing and shocking scenes that I have ever laid eyes on, but quick decisions had to be made to save the lives of the soldiers and there was no room for emotion.

We were specifically instructed by the government not to write about or take photographs of any casualties regardless of how unusual the case may be. I remember when one of my colleagues took a photograph of a severely crushed hand. Within hours an officer from Military Information had turned up, taken the camera from his hand, thrown it on the floor and stamped on it. He destroyed the camera and the film and made it very clear that anybody who tried to break the rules would risk severe punishment. It was obvious that one of the loyal soldiers had reported him to Military Information.

For most of the injuries I saw, a camera was not needed; the images were so disturbing that they were etched on my brain and have stayed with me my entire life. Below are just a few of the casualties that I can bring myself to talk about.

CASE ONE

The 8th February was an Iraqi national holiday and also my daughter May's birthday. To celebrate the two occasions, and being off work from the hospital, Mary and I planned a family holiday at the Alhabania Resort.

Originally Alhabania was a British airbase until 1958 when the Iraqi revolution and the coup against the King happened, and the British vacated the area. Alhabania had a beautiful, enormous lake that took its water high up from the Euphrates as it entered Iraqi land from Syria. On the vast expanse of land around the lake, the government built a lovely holiday resort of hotels and self-contained villas. All were exquisitely designed and furnished, scattered amongst luxury landscaped gardens. There were numerous swimming pools and recreation facilities around. Saddam had built himself one of the most imposing houses in the area, designed for him by French architects.

Early in the morning of 8th February 1981, having already packed our cases, we loaded the car ready for our journey to Baghdad, and then the 150km on to Alhabania. As we were about to lock the house and leave, the telephone rang, and I wish we had never answered it. Mary rushed to answer the phone and called me to speak to the Managing Director of the Health Service in Babylon.

'Ismaiel,' he said, 'you need to go now to the Province of Al Hashimia'.

This was a small village about ten miles away from the centre of Hilla.

'What for?' I replied. 'You know very well that I am off duty and I am just about to go to Alhabania with my wife and daughter'.

'Well,' he replied, 'This is a military order'.

Reluctant to go, I asked him if he knew what was going on and who the order came from. He told me that the order had come from the Chief of Staff and that they were not prepared to discuss anything over the phone.

'What can I do in that village?' I asked. 'If they have a surgical problem then they should send the patient to Al Jamhori Hospital in Babylon'.

The Managing Director got very irritated with me and said, 'Ismaiel, don't waste my time. This is an order and I strongly advise you go now. I am sending a private vehicle, please get yourself ready.'

I told him not to send me a car as my own would be more comfortable and much faster than a hospital ambulance. Mary had realised by this point that our holiday was going to be disrupted, but as usual she was very supportive of my work and very understanding. She encouraged me and urged me to go as soon as possible with her usual advice for me to stay calm, not to criticise anybody and not to get angry. With this advice I would always be sent off with a kiss, a sandwich and a can of coke! Mary always got her own way and knew as well as I did the dangers involved in refusing military orders.

I arrived at Al Hashimia within thirty-five minutes; it was on the main road between Hilla and Alkut. At the entrance to the village there was a small health centre, which looked more like sanatorium for management of surgical conditions than a hospital.

As I pulled up I saw a huge crowd of military cars and artillery vehicles. Soldiers were all over the place and on the side of the road there were two burnt-out military lorries. The road was closed and all cars were being diverted away from the area. When I introduced myself they allowed me to go through and rushed me to drive straight to the sanatorium.

I walked in amid a very big crowd of military personnel and was shown to a large waiting room, which was packed with high-ranking officers and marshals. I had absolutely no idea what was going on. A military officer that I didn't know – but that had the largest amount of gold that I had ever seen sitting on his shoulder – turned to me.

'Dr Ismaiel, this is a top secret incident. We had a convoy moving from a camp near Babylon on its way to support the war front. Our lorries were carrying heavy loads of bombs and ammunition. As we arrived at the village of Al Hashimia, our convoy came under very heavy fire from the many orchards adjacent to the main road. We responded to their fire and within ten minutes we were in full control of the situation. Unfortunately the insurgents escaped and we lost lives and a large amount of ammunition. They seem to have targeted the lorries that were loaded with explosives and all the personnel inside have been burned to death; all but one'.

He stood up, took me by the arm and led me to another room within the sanatorium. The guard on the door opened it as he saw the officer arriving. On the floor there were around thirty dead bodies, as black as charcoal. The majority of them were missing limbs; most of them didn't have a head. In another corner of the room there was a heap of limbs and heads, I guessed they were saving them to make up a complete body for their relatives to bury, although in reality it would be impossible to identify which charred limbs belonged to which body and they would no doubt send any corpse with any of the limbs.

'Doctor,' he said to me, 'those are the victims, those are the martyrs. Those are the good, loyal Iraqis who have been killed for no reason by a bloody traitor. We are lucky to have one person still alive. He is in a severe state of shock and badly injured, but we have kept him alive through direct blood transfusions from other soldiers. We need you to save his life, as he is the only one that might have any information about how this incident happened. He might have seen the people who shot at them; he may be the most important link to the whole incident'.

The high-ranking officer took me into a small restricted room about three metres long and three metres wide. It had clearly been used as a minor operating theatre. It contained a mobile projector, very basic surgical equipment and a simple autoclave sterilizer. I guessed it was used by the nurses who ran the sanatorium for simple suturing of superficial wounds. They also had a very basic and outdated operating table.

I was told by the Charge Nurse there that on occasions when they had a medical officer with surgical skills or interests they used this room to operate on simple cases such as hernia repairs. He told me that for the last six months they had not had a surgical practice and all cases had been transferred to Hilla.

In the middle of the crowd lay a soldier on an operating table. He was in severe shock from blood loss. He had dressings and bandages covering his abdomen, completely soaked with blood.

'Who was the medical personnel accompanying this military convoy?' I asked.

Two men stepped forward. A young, nervous military Doctor, looking absolutely lost, introduced himself 'Dr Ahmed, sir'. The second was a bright man, dressed in theatre blues, introduced himself as an Operating Theatre Assistant specialising in anaesthetics, his name was Salah.

'Would everybody else who is non-medical or not of a nursing background please leave the room and stand by to help when needed,' I said.

The room was evacuated apart from the Chief of Staff who stayed with me to oversee the procedure. I introduced myself to the injured solider, who was not in any position to respond, but I explained that I was going to undo his dressings to see the wound.

There was massive trauma to the abdominal wall. There was a big ragged abdominal injury just above his belly button; his abdomen had a large piece of spiky and irregular shaped shrapnel wedged into it. He also had other less severe superficial injuries all over his body. It was a massive trauma and the shrapnel could have done very severe damage inside. If we removed it we were likely to find ourselves in a surgical emergency that we might not be able to deal with there. There were no lights, surgical instruments or anaesthetic cover and I suggested that we transfer him to Al Jamhori Hospital in Hilla.

'We had contemplated that actually Doctor,' the Chief of Staff said, 'but we thought that he might not make it in the transfer and we cannot risk losing him. That's why we called you in'.

The Anaesthetic Assistant, with great confidence, said that he had an anaesthetic machine in the mobile ambulance unit and was more than happy to entubate and ventilate the patient during transfer. He added that he had anaesthetised a lot of difficult cases and he felt that the patient's breathing was deteriorating since the incident.

'Get all your equipment here please and be ready,' I said to him. 'Do we have enough blood?' I asked.

'Unlimited, Sir,' he responded, 'although we have been doing the cross matching in a very primitive way. We have been using a matchstick on a glass slide to assess compatibility. We have had no other way'. As we were deciding what to do, the anaesthetist, Salah, turned to me.

'Excuse me Sir, I think we are losing him. His breathing is deteriorating and I can't hear any air going into his chest. I'm going to intubate and ventilate him'.

With the machine from the mobile unit ready he immediately intubated the patient and controlled his breathing, but unfortunately the patient continued to be in a severe state of shock from the huge amount of blood loss. I realised that there was no way he was going to make it to the hospital in Hilla. Without any hesitation I found myself in a world of my own.

'Get me theatre gowns,' I shouted. 'I need at least three assistants and all the available surgical equipment you can find, and let us pray to God that we can open him here. Everybody who is not a medic leave the room now'.

The Chief Of Staff went outside and wished us the best of luck. Within five minutes I had slipped into theatre clothes and two Charge Nurses came in to help me and the young military Doctor. I cleaned the soldier's abdominal wall with normal saline; I took a knife and slit his abdomen up and down before removing the impacted metal shrapnel. It was horrible, irregular and had very sharp spikes. As I took it away I was able to see the damaged organs underneath.

There was a huge hole in his stomach, which I quickly trimmed and sutured. Blood was welling out of his abdomen; his transverse colon was macerated so I resected it between clamps and gave him a colostomy. His left kidney was completely damaged and he was bleeding from his spleen as well, so I removed them both. I did everything within less than forty minutes but the patient was still losing vast amounts of blood and was quite unstable.

I opened the abdominal cavity like a book and asked for a handheld torch to see it more clearly. Looking into the abdomen, with the three assistants retracting as hard as they could, gave me ample visual access and I could see that there was nothing missing. Higher up in the cavity there was blood pouring from a big hole in his left diaphragm, so I pushed my right hand up into the chest and felt an orange sized piece of metal shrapnel which seemed to have impacted at the root of the lung, where all the important blood vessels and the air pipe come in and out of the left lung.

I extended the incision to the left side of his chest and opened it widely, which was a much easier procedure than opening the abdomen. I asked my assistants to hold the ribs apart and there I found a large piece of shrapnel sitting on the main blood supply to the lung. He was lucky that the shrapnel had not hit his heart or aorta. I removed the shrapnel and blood poured out from his pulmonary artery. I put a clamp across the root of the lung, on the blood vessels and the bronchus.

'Well done Sir,' the anaesthetist exclaimed. 'His oxygenation level is rising and he is getting some colour in his nose and lips. I can feel his pulse and feeble blood pressure'.

I quickly removed the left lung and tied the vessels and the bronchus securely. I washed the chest and abdomen out with plenty of saline. Fifteen minutes went by and the patient's blood pressure was rising, his pulse volume improving and we seemed to have done the job. Whether the patient would make it to an uncomplicated recovery or not was left to be seen.

I had done all I could do in these conditions. I closed the abdomen and chest in a very quick and basic way. I stayed in the room until the anaesthetist had assured me one hundred percent that the patient was stable. He had to stay on the machine until his transfer to Hilla. I left theatre feeling like a hero because everybody around me showered me with praise for my quick and innovative thinking.

The Chief of Staff had been continuously updated and when I left theatre he shook my hand and told one of the lower ranked officers to inform Headquarters in Baghdad that the operation was successful.

'Sir' I said, 'you must understand that the actual practical part of the operation was successful, but you have seen for yourself that we have performed this massive operation in very primitive and basic surroundings. The patient may suffer lethal consequences. Let us move him to Hilla quickly and I will get the Intensive Care Unit ready for him now.'

When the ambulance arrived in Hilla the Mayor of the town, the highest members of the Ba'ath party and the Chief of Al-Amin were waiting at the hospital. We transferred the patient to the Intensive Care Unit and he remained stable. As I left the ICU the entire operation played back in my mind. I couldn't believe what I had done and felt a sense of pride that it had been successful. They don't teach you how to deal with these situations in medical school, yet instinct clearly took over.

Within a short time the Deputy of Defence Minister arrived at the hospital. He came to see me after he visited the patient in the Intensive Care Unit.

'Doctor,' he said, 'his Excellency, the Minister of Defence, wants to speak to you on the phone'.

He handed me a military phone on which he had already dialled the number.

'God bless you and your loved ones Doctor,' the Minister said in a very warm and calm voice. 'I heard what you did for this man. We really needed him to stay alive, as he was the only witness to the incident. When he recovers enough and is able to talk I would like to come and see both of you in Hilla.'

'Thank you sir,' I said. 'I did my duty and my best within the given circumstances. I hope he makes it. The next few days are going to be very critical'.

'Don't worry,' the Minister of Defence joked. 'He is Iraqi and the Iraqis are stronger than any infection! This man is a fighter and believe me our bodies are immune by nature. He will make it.'

I went home. Mary was awake, waiting up for me to hear the story. It had been nearly twenty-four hours since I had left her. A few days later, at lunchtime, the local Military Chief of Staff in the Infantry Military Camp invited me to his office for a cup of tea. I arrived there to find that he had arranged a big lunch and had invited both military and Ba'ath party members. When we finished our lunch and sat for a cup of tea he was full of praise about my help and assistance, and with the operation I had carried out for the surviving soldier.

'The Minister of Defence had promised to visit the patient and yourself at the hospital but due to his commitments he was unable to do so. He has asked me to thank you on his behalf'.

He walked over to his desk and took out a lovely small, carved wooden box and handed it to me.

'Open it,' he said, 'and see if you like it'.

The box was lined with red velvet and inside was the most beautiful 9 mm caliber silver Browning pistol, accompanied by a formal license. This gun was only carried by the highest-ranking people in the government, including President Saddam himself. In war time it was customary and quite a high honour to present somebody with a gun or a sword. It was a very prestigious gift.

On every occasion such as Eid or Christmas, the solider I had saved, along with his family, would come from Baghdad to visit us and would always bring with them two live lambs, fresh food and gold for my daughters.

I once went to see him and his family at their home in Al Karrada in Baghdad. To see the happiness of his large family, living in a beautiful old Arabic style house, was very satisfying. The solider had called over his wife, who was carrying a little baby boy in her arms.

'My son, Doctor Ismaiel, I have named him after you. Ismaiel is a name I never want to forget.'

Visiting him in his home and seeing his family made me very emotional, knowing that although I had been angry at missing my family holiday, I had changed their lives forever.

CASE TWO

In 1982, whilst I was serving at Omara Hospital, we experienced one of the Iranian's most vicious attacks during what we later called the Albesatin Fight. It was named after the section of Iranian land where the fighting had taken place, which was about forty kilometres from Omara Hospital.

We had been warned a few hours before to expect a high number of serious casualties with evacuations coming to Omara Hospital. We began to prepare ourselves by dividing into groups, each in charge of a location within the hospital. Any team not on official duty was put on high alert in case they were needed, to ensure availability of all specialties in surgery.

The Hospital Director had received information from Baghdad that more medical help was on its way to Omara. When waiting for something to happen we normally sat in the Director's room, chatting and laughing, as it was an opportunity to meet colleagues from other parts of Iraq whom we had not seen for a while. We would never receive information regarding military matters and therefore had no idea when to expect the evacuations to happen. We would simply sit and wait for first ambulance to arrive.

At about 8pm on a scorching summer day in 1982 all hell broke loose. A convoy of buses being used as ambulances queued outside the hospital along with helicopters and military cars, transporting casualties from the war zone.

Hundreds of blood-soaked soldiers began filling the hospital corridors, casualties left on the floor and in any available space in the hospital, including the hospital garden. We had already organised our work so that each surgical team had military junior Doctors and each team was responsible for a different section of the hospital. Therefore all the casualties in a particular area were the responsibility of a specific team.

On that day I had been put in charge of the injured soldiers in the garden. With a junior Doctor, I began moving quickly between the stretchers, trying to assess and triage the injured soldiers and the urgency and seriousness of their condition. The junior Doctor would write down the name of a soldier, his military number and underneath a list of his major injuries and the treatment required. We moved quickly, writing short and informative notes about every soldier. We would arrange the theatre list accordingly, prioritising those that needed life-saving operations and allocating the best surgeon to the case.

The scene that day was horrific. The soldiers were brave and tolerant and didn't beg for preferential treatment. Although they were visibly in severe pain from their injuries, they seemed to be distracted by their extreme thirst and this seemed to be their main priority. The only cries that I could hear were for water. Most of the soldiers would have been fighting in the blistering heat of the desert for four days without even a sip of water. Of course, all the medical staff were busy going through the cases, trying to prioritise urgent surgery and see to the horrific injuries.

While I was assessing a group of injured soldiers in the garden, an unbelievable sight caught my eye. Across the courtyard lay a severely wounded soldier who had been put on intravenous saline (IV). I watched as he slowly brought himself to his feet, disconnected the rubber tube from his vein and moved towards one of the soldiers lying next to him. He put the tube to the soldier's mouth and let him drink the saline; blood pouring from his arm as he did so. He then put the tube back into his vein and stumbled onto another soldier to do the same.

I had never seen such desperation and such kindness in a time of war. Most of these men were suffering from internal bleeding, loss of limbs and damaged organs, yet the severe thirst they suffered from had numbed their pain. As I looked on I realised that he was doing more for these men at that moment than I could ever have done for them as a Doctor.

CASE THREE

Our duties as Doctors were to look after the injured soldiers, regardless of whether they were Iraqi or Iranian. The injured Iranian soldiers were brought into a secured area known as the hospital prison. The ward was no different to any other in the hospital apart from the fact that it was locked and guarded, which was only natural at a time of war.

One day, I had finished my duties in the garden area and was called to the hospital prison to look at some patients that had just been brought in from the frontline. I entered the ward and there were over twenty soldiers, all looking surprisingly well considering what they had been through.

All the cases were simple and trivial injuries that could be attended to by the junior Doctors. I knew that most of the soldiers had been brought in as prisoners of war, in order to elicit security information from them.

The Charge Nurse on the ward came over and told me that there was a young Iranian boy who may need attention. He was sitting upright in his bed, absolutely silent. His face was emotionless. He had refused to eat or drink anything that was offered to him. He was so young that he had no facial hair. I guessed that he was about fourteen years old.

The Charge Nurse whispered to me to take a look at his lower limbs, so I approached the young boy and greeted him in an Arabic way: *'Alsalamo alaykum'*. I knew that he understood my greeting, but he did not respond to it, his face was still expressionless. Through a translator I asked if he had any pain and the response was 'no'. I then asked him if I could examine his lower limbs and he didn't react, but he didn't refuse. The nurse gently pulled back the bedcover and I moved forward to examine him.

What I saw under those sheets was so disturbing that it made me feel physically sick. His lower limbs had been completely flattened by a tank. They had become nothing more than a flat sheet of dead black human tissue. There was no bleeding and I couldn't identify a single bone or muscle to examine. His limbs were no longer identifiable as legs; it was as if somebody had attached a flat sheet of fabric to his thighs.

He calmly told me that he had fallen over and a tank had driven over his legs, its chain had crushed his limbs against the sand leaving him unable to move. He told me that he was brought straight into the prison. I wasn't sure exactly how the boy was still alive let alone how he was sitting up in bed without flinching in pain. He must have gone so far beyond the depths of pain that his body had shut down altogether.

I asked the translator to explain to the boy that he would need urgent and immediate bilateral above-knee amputations, making it very clear that this was the only way to save his life. If we didn't, necrotic tissue would travel into his circulation in a matter of time and kill him. The boy outright refused to have surgery. He told me that he had joined the Army not simply to fight but to achieve martyrdom.

'If you save my life,' he said, 'then I won't go to heaven, and I have the key to heaven'.

He lifted his shirt to show me a huge metal key hanging on a chain around his neck.

'If you want to operate to save my life so that I can live in this dreadful, meaningless life then I don't want it. I want to die as soon as possible.'

The young boy got his wish and died twenty-four hours later; what brainwashing and what a waste of a life.

CASE FOUR

Lying on one of the stretchers in the corridor of the hospital was a very quiet Iraqi Colonel. His uniform was ripped and stained with dried blood; his head was completely wrapped in bandages. From a distance it looked as though he had a large snowball sitting on his shoulders. He lay in the corridor leading to theatre where there was a hot debate between a group of Doctors about timing of his operation. There was another patient, who was a prisoner of war bleeding heavily from his injury to his face.

At that moment every surgeon was busy and the debate was around who the maxillofacial surgeon should deal with first. Apparently the Colonel was still able to hear his surroundings. When he wanted to communicate, he used hand signals to request a pen and paper.

He wrote 'I am well. Don't worry about me, save the life of the prisoner, he may have important information'

Even at a time of immense suffering and pain the Colonel wanted to demonstrate his loyalty to Saddam and the regime. When the Colonel's turn came to go to theatre I insisted on being there as I was intrigued by his facial injuries. He was given anaesthesia through a hole in his windpipe, which had already been created by the paramedics when they evacuated him. The anaesthetist simply replaced the small tube with a larger one and started providing anaesthetic.

When the maxillofacial surgeon started cutting away the bandages the sight was horrific. The Colonel didn't have a face. He had massively swollen and bruised eyes but below them nothing. No nose, no lips, no chin, no jawbone. He had half a tongue and a few teeth at the back of his mouth.

We were told that a rocket passed him at face level and had taken off the front of his face, miraculously leaving him with an intact brain. There was no major bleeding and all the small vessels had clotted by the time he was rescued. The quick-thinking frontline Doctors had inserted a tube into his neck, to maintain his breathing, before wrapping his face with bandages.

The appearance of his face was difficult to stomach, and the fact that he was still alive was even more shocking. There was nothing the Maxillofacial surgeon could do, so he washed the wounds, reported all the injuries in detail, documented them in a medical report and dressed his face. A helicopter took him straight from Omara Hospital to Al-Rashid Military Hospital in Baghdad.

Out of curiosity, I followed his case, wanting to know how he would continue with his life. It turned out that only a few hours after he arrived in Baghdad, he was flown in a private jet to France for plastic surgery. This was his reward for his loyalty to Saddam. He spent nearly six months in Paris having numerous plastic surgery repairs before returning home alive and well.

Saddam Hussein was personally in touch with the officer whilst he was in France and sent updates to his family back home. Saddam eventually appointed Delshad, the Colonel, as a very high-ranking officer in the Ministry of Defence for the remaining years of the Iran/Iraq war.

CASE FIVE

While I was at Omara Hospital in 1983 there was another bout of very heavy fighting in what was called Al-Kafajia, a place inside the Iranian border. When the fighting stopped for a few hours the two sides started clearing the casualties.

The ambulance team were instructed to give priority to evacuating soldiers whose injuries were definitely salvageable and to leave behind those that were hopeless cases. The ambulances therefore picked soldiers who had an imminent risk to the viability of their tissue or organs, or if their life was at risk from a salvageable injury.

Injured soldiers who were standing on their feet and managing their injuries were given simple first aid at the scene and left until the second or third wave of evacuations. This form of triage was never accurate; in the middle of a warzone with thousands of injured soldiers, mistakes were definitely made.

It was 21st September 1983, my birthday. I was quite happy to be working as I was one year wiser and in what I felt was an enviable position, helping people in desperate need. I would always look at the injured soldiers and try to picture them amongst their families; their mothers, fathers, wives, children, brothers and sisters, many of whom would be desperately waiting for the return of their loved one. I always imagined the family sitting in their garden having their afternoon tea with cold water and melon, joking and chatting but missing those members of the family that were fighting at the front.

There would have been no way for them to know where their loved ones were at any given moment in time. If they died they would never know the circumstances of the death. They could have little idea of the experience and the suffering they had been through. The bravery of the soldier – and his loyalty to his country – would be buried with him. I felt responsible for their lives. I didn't want to imagine the family opening the door to a wooden box on their doorstep. I felt that even if I could save a life knowing that the soldier would be left with a disability then at least they would still have a long recovery period with their family, and they would have stories to tell. I knew that all the soldiers would definitely remember one name, and that would be of the surgeon who saved them.

Doing an on-call shift on my birthday, I was triaging the casualties in my geographical territory within the hospital. I was in the garden again; this was my favourite patch because there were normally more casualties sent to the garden, meaning more lives could be saved. It was also enjoyable to practice medicine in the open air.

Making his way through the hundreds of injured soldiers on stretchers, a soldier stumbled into the garden. Barefoot, he was on the verge of collapsing with exhaustion. As he walked towards me I could see that he was holding a dirty pillowcase tight to his waistline, covering his abdomen. The pillowcase appeared to be full of something and every now and then he peeped into the sack before holding it back tightly against his waist.

'Hey you, soldier, come here, what are you doing?' I called over to him in a deliberately relaxed tone of voice. 'How can we help you? I am a surgeon.'

He had a very likeable smile and a friendly face. I was thinking that there was nothing seriously wrong with him.

'Have a seat under this tree where there is a cooler breeze and tell me what is wrong'.

I asked if he was thirsty and ordered one of the hospital staff to bring him a glass of cold water.

'I can't sit down Sir,' he said. 'If you don't mind I will lie down. I've not slept for twenty-four hours'.

'Okay,' I said, 'please yourself'. Tell me what's in the pillowcase. What are you hiding?'

'My intestines, Sir,' he replied casually.

I couldn't believe what I was hearing so I squatted next to him to take a look. He carefully and gradually removed the pillowcase. His entire small bowel was inside the pillowcase; it had protruded through a wound in his abdominal wall. Funnily enough, the bowel looked healthy and well-hydrated. I asked him for his name and military number as identification. I then asked him to explain what exactly had happened and how he had got here.

'Well, Sir,' he said, 'we were asleep when a counter-attack began from the Iranian side. It was awful. They used every possible weapon and a very large number of soldiers in an attempt to defeat us and push us out of Al-Kafajia. We resisted for a while but eventually, after about twelve hours of heavy fighting, both sides stopped for reorganisation and evacuation of the injured.

I left my bunker with two other soldiers and as we got out a bomb exploded in front of us. Two of my friends died instantly but I thought that I was fine. I didn't feel any pain or see any blood. I rushed back to the bunker but nobody else was there. I picked up some of my possessions to prepare for a retreat. I went out again to inspect the war field, to check on my comrades. I suddenly felt damp around my belt line. I lifted my shirt, which had been ripped by the explosion, and only then did I realise that I had been hit by shrapnel from the bomb and there was a ragged hole just underneath my belly button. It was leaking some blood and yellowish fluid.

I went over to the ambulance staff that had arrived but they were too busy with other casualties that looked much more serious than me. I tried to show them the wound but they didn't look interested, so cleaned it for me and gave me a bandage to wrap around my waist. They told me I was lucky it wasn't serious or deep and to sit aside until they had sorted out the others. So I sat down, waiting to be evacuated in the next round.

Two hours later, out of the blue, they started to attack again, with extensive ground missiles and shooting. We were ordered to retreat back using any means of transport. Soldiers started jumping on the back of trucks and lorries, but I wasn't lucky enough to get a place or a lift. Everybody was fighting to get onto a vehicle.

Our Chief shouted to those who could not get transport to run and to look for the nearest safe shelter. With other soldiers

I started running. After a while I felt something pop out of my stomach, pushing the dressing forwards. Very soon the bandage got wet and came undone but I continued running until I realised that there was something protruding out of the wound. I stopped and looked down and saw about two feet of my bowel hanging out.

I couldn't do anything so kept running while holding it in my hands. Gradually more and more loops of the bowel started coming out until it became very heavy and difficult for me to contain within my two hands. I called in to one of the small camps, looking for a sheet to wrap my intestines in. Nobody was there so I helped myself to the nearest pillowcase from a deserted bunker. I put my entire protruded bowel into it and held it tight around my waist.

I tried to hitchhike whenever I saw any military cars or ambulances passing me but nobody stopped for me. I continued walking towards Omara. It was scorching hot so I regularly inspecting my bowel and noticed that it was becoming very dry and had begun sticking to the pillowcase. I decided that the only way to keep it damp was to pour water over it from the river and marshes that I passed. When I finally got to the outskirts of Omara a civilian car stopped for me and gave me a lift to the hospital.'

The soldier told me he had walked for twelve hours, holding his intestines in a pillowcase. Stunned, I asked one of the junior Doctors to take him to theatre, clean his bowels with saline and push them back inside. I asked him to make sure that there were no internal injuries to the bowel. The junior Doctor told me that he had to go and find an available anaesthetist to give the soldier a general anaesthetic. The soldier jumped at the sound of general anaesthesia.

'No sir please, I don't want general anaesthetic. I don't want to die. I survived the bombing and I have survived this injury, something might go wrong under anaesthetic. I have four children that I haven't seen for three months. I want to see my wife, my children and my mum and dad. Please just put my bowel back into my abdomen and give me a sick note to let me go home. I don't need anaesthetic, I can push them back in but I don't know how to stitch up my abdomen. Please sir, just ask your Doctor to clean the bowel for me thoroughly, push it back into the abdomen and let him stitch my abdomen without any anaesthetic. I don't mind the pain. I just want to leave the hospital quickly.'

I felt his request was illogical in the circumstances. I tried to advise him against it, but failed. I told the junior Doctor to take him to casualty, clean his bowel with saline, check for injuries and stitch his abdomen with a few nylon stitches, using local anaesthetic infiltration to the abdominal wall. I gave him a sick note for thirty days and told him that when he got home he should go to the local hospital. I advised that he might need a CT scan.

He asked me if I was from the Sayed Bhayah family in Babylon. When I confirmed that I was, a big satisfied smile appeared on his face.

'Putting your blessed hands on me is the best medicine Sir,' he said quietly. 'I don't need a CT scan, I don't need antibiotics and I certainly don't need anaesthesia'.

Within an hour his abdomen was washed and sutured and he came looking for me. He insisted on kissing my hand and said goodbye with tears of happiness in his eyes. I took his arm and led him away from everybody, walking out to the garden. When we were alone I put my hand in my pocket and took out a £50 note, putting it in his hand. Embarrassed, he refused, but when I asked him if he had any money on him, he looked at me.

'No wonder people treat your family with such respect,' he said. 'You are angels, Sir, you are no ordinary human being. I don't have a cent on me'.

He leant on my hand, kissed it and disappeared out of the hospital.

About a month later, I was in Hilla, in the centre of Babylon. We were having lunch on a Friday afternoon in our garden. It was nice weather for October. The doorbell rang and our housemaid opened the door; she came back to say that somebody wanted to see me outside.

I went to the door and it was my patient, his father, his mother, his wife and all his children. They were all sitting in a double pick-up truck, and in the back was a huge black and white cow. After the usual greeting all of them kissed my hand. His father went down to kiss my shoes, but I stopped him and the others from doing so. I gave them all an Arabic welcoming hug. They led the cow, which at the time was worth at least £1,000, into the garden and tied it to a tree. They then went back to the truck and started taking out other gifts of vegetables, fruit, homemade cheese and two geese for the children.

This was a very traditional present in Iraq from our patients. I invited them all in and Mary gave them tea and cake with fruit, soft drinks and sweets for the children. When my daughters, May, who was then four years-old, and Hannah, who was two, came out to the garden the whole family queued to kiss their hands for blessing.

I asked Hassan to tell me his story since he left Omara.

'Well, Sir,' he said, 'I hope you won't be angry with me. I arrived at Karbala and went straight to see my family. They were over the moon that I was alive. We spent the whole night eating and chatting. I was the happiest man on earth to be with them again'.

He told me that he slept all of the following day and then went to see a specialist in the town later that week. The specialist told him that if he had anything seriously wrong he would have been dead by now. However, the specialist did advise Hassan to return the following day for a CT scan and antibiotics. He never went for the CT scan. Instead he took his family to the holy shrine of Imam Al Hussain, the grandson of Prophet Mohammed, buried in Karbala.

The Shi'ite people in Iraq believed that the shrine of Imam Al Hussain in Karbala held more healing powers than any medicine. Before they went to leave, I showed them to their car and Hassan put his hand in his pocket, got out a £50 note and put it in my hand.

'I cannot repay your kindness, Sir, but I can easily return the £50.'

CASE SIX

In the final months of 1984, I was based at the Northern Frontier Hospital in the village of Mandali, a very small town northeast of Baghdad and around five kilometres from the border with Iran. It was a very small, old hospital that had recently been refurbished and was equipped with excellent facilities. This was the least busy frontier during the war; the heaviest fighting would usually occur in Omara and Basra. During the entire eight year war I was only sent to Mandali twice.

When I arrived there in November 1984, our driver took us directly to the Doctors' accommodation. There were five Doctors already in the house, one orthopaedic surgeon, two anaesthetists and two general surgeons. Normally there was an overlap between Doctors of the same speciality to avoid having a gap in any one particular speciality. My counterpart surgeon was due to go back to his hometown the following day. We introduced ourselves to each other and began chatting about work and how bored we had been with the lack of heavy casualties. After lunch we had some tea and fresh fruit before asking our driver to take us to the hospital to meet the team.

It was a pretty small hospital with a twin theatre and a total of 120 beds. The Casualty department had been properly refurbished and enlarged to accommodate a significant number of casualties. The few houses in the vicinity of the hospital had been evacuated before undergoing alternations to make them suitable to accommodate patients in times of heavy fighting.

Dr Ibrahim, the surgeon I was replacing, introduced me to the hospital staff. Later that afternoon, when I had returned to the house, we had an emergency call from the hospital. We were told that a patient had come in with a missile injury. When Dr Ibrahim and I arrived back at the hospital we found a big military crowd had surrounded the hospital with their cars, tanks and lorries. The place was heaving with officers and soldiers, and all the patients had been evacuated into the garden. We asked what was going on and one of the officers led us inside the hospital and straight into theatre. Neither of us had prepared ourselves for what we were about to find.

A fully conscious soldier lay on the operating table holding his hands over a large metal object protruding from his abdomen. He showed no signs of fear or pain. As I moved in to take a closer look, I was pulled back by a member of staff.

'It's an unexploded missile, sir,' they whispered in my ear

Apparently, the soldier had been asleep in his bunker, when an Austrian 175mm missile fell through the roof and fell onto the soldier, but failed to explode. It smashed through the roof and landed on his stomach, where he held it steady.

Before it is launched this missile is 17.5cm at its widest diameter and has a total length of 90cm. It is made up of a brass base filled with explosives and an alloy head, which is also full of explosives. The metal alloy head looked exactly like a large bullet. It should have hit a solid surface in order to explode and release the jagged shrapnel within it, causing hundreds of casualties. However, it was currently lodged into the abdomen of the patient who lay before me, and it was my job to remove it.

Within minutes, piles of sandbags were carefully lined up inside the operating theatre, from the floor to the ceiling, to provide protection against an explosion. However, that was protection only for those on the other side of the wall. Unexpectedly, the pressure of the situation did not hit me. My heart rate was increasing rapidly but I couldn't help but think to myself that this had more to do with the excitement of the operation at hand than the danger that threatened us; I always looked for a challenge.

We asked everybody to leave the room apart from the bomb expert from the Engineering Division, and our surgical team. The bomb expert stayed in theatre, waiting for us to remove the missile head from the patient's abdomen before he could disarm it outside the hospital. Both Ibrahim and I scrubbed up and asked one of the Charge Nurses to firmly hold the missile whilst the patient was put to sleep by the anaesthetist. I was left in charge of the operation as Dr Ibrahim was leaving the following day.

As soon as the patient was anaesthetised, I washed the abdomen around the missile and asked if everybody was ready for us to lift it. I stood with clamps in my hands, anticipating that there would be an immediate vascular injury with catastrophic bleeding. In the abdomen there are two very important major blood vessels, the aorta, which is the main artery in the body, and the inferior vena cava, the main vein through

The Hanging Gardens of Babylon

which all the blood from the lower limbs returns back to the heart. These run side by side along the back of the abdomen. I asked Ibrahim to help the others lift the missile out of the abdomen gently and slowly and not to rotate or tilt it. They slowly lifted it and within seconds it was disengaged from his stomach.

He was left with an enormous gaping hole in his abdominal wall; I very quickly enlarged the area by cutting it open further and opening it up like a book. I assessed his abdomen and was shocked to find that he had no serious complications inside. No excessive bleeding, no bowel content leak and no loose faecal matter. I immediately calmed down and started washing the abdomen out with a large amount of saline whilst the missile was carried outside. His small and large bowels were massively bruised, especially at its mesentery; the fatty tissue apron from which the bowel hangs and which contains all of the blood supply to the bowel. There had clearly been some bleeding from the mesentery, but this had stopped on its own.

The left kidney was badly bruised but there was no urine leakage or bleeding from it and nothing to indicate that it was not viable, so I assured myself that both kidneys would be fine to stay. Then Ibrahim and I inspected all of his abdominal organs and found nothing but clotted blood. He had no major vascular or visceral damage. I tidied the abdominal wall wound and closed him up.

The following day the patient was conscious and stable and in very high spirits, asking when he could go home to see his family. Not once did he allude to his bravery or complain about the pain. When I asked him how he had managed to keep calm while holding the missile against his body he asked me what I would have done if I were in his place.

Had he not remained calm and held the missile still, not only would he have suffered the most painful death, but also would have killed hundreds of his fellow comrades. I felt rewarded that I had had the most interesting casualty of the week and probably of a lifetime. I spent the rest of the week in Mandali with nothing more than a few minor injuries to treat and a couple of appendectomies.

CASE SEVEN

Mohammed was one of the Charge Nurses in our hospital in Babylon. We got on very well at work, so I employed him to help me with my private practice in the afternoons. A handsome man with blue eyes and blond hair, he was extremely well mannered, which made him a joy to work with. Married with three children, Mohammed was very well-spoken and widely educated. I looked after him very well in return for his dedication and loyalty.

In 1984, Mohammed was sent back to the army by the government who had started calling on the Reserve Army, as there was a desperate shortage of soldiers. The death toll of young and middle-aged men had escalated on both sides. The main graveyard for Sheas was in Najaf, south of Baghdad. Although it has always been the biggest graveyard in the world, even before the Iraq-Iran war, it was now overpopulated with the dead. It was quite a common sight to see the cars carrying the coffins of their loved ones queuing at the entrance of the graveyard for hours before they had a chance to bury them in peace. My Charge Nurse, Mohammed, handed over his duties in my hospital and said farewell to his family before going to the front.

One day in 1985 I was on-call in Omara. There were no acute casualties or evacuations apart from very sporadic cases of bullet injuries, infected wounds and sniper shots; about twenty to thirty such cases would show up in an eight hour shift. When I became exhausted I would let the junior Doctor do the easier cases while I rested in the Hospital Director's room, eating and drinking. When I was needed, one of the Casualty nurses would either ring his office or call for me personally.

At about 7 p.m. I got called by one of the Doctors to see an interesting case. The junior Doctor exclaimed that he had never heard of such a case before and he wanted me to review the patient and give my opinion.

On our walk down to Casualty, I asked the Doctor what we had to deal with. 'Small fish, Sir,' he said and laughed.

Confused by his comment I headed for cubicle 6, pulled back the curtain and came face to face with Mohammed. He was lying on a couch on his side, which gave away the fact that he had injured his buttocks. The sight of the soldier unfazed me due to the terrors of war my eyes had met before. I casually greeted him and asked what the problem was.

'Well, Sir,' he said in an almost embarrassed manner, 'my buttock was eaten by small fish in the marshes. The Iranians began an unexpected heavy attack. We were caught off guard and ran for our lives. It was chaos. Some were captured, others killed, a few escaped. The Iranians were shooting at anything that moved. I ran into the marshes and decided to play dead. I tore up a piece of cane, put it in my mouth and put my head face down in the water, floating like a dead man. I had to keep absolutely motionless as I could hear the splashes of the Iranian soldiers walking close to me, looking for Iraqi soldiers. I kept absolutely still.'

He continued his story and told me that small fish started gathering around him, biting and munching inside his trousers from the belt area downwards. They seemed to have gotten an appetite for his buttocks. Hundreds of these fish were eating away at his flesh but he could not move because his life was at stake. It was a choice between being taken as a prisoner of war and being tortured and killed, or letting the fish enjoy their meal.

Mohammed was very thirsty and had no choice but to drink the marsh water while he was there. The only thing going through his mind at the time was his wife and children. He said he could picture them receiving his dead body and having to spend the rest of their lives without him. This had given him great emotional and physical strength to fight for survival.

He decided that he needed to stay alive, even if the fish ate his lower limbs. His mental strength overpowered his pain threshold. Mohammed lay there for twenty-four hours. When he was sure that the Iranians had cleared the area, he slowly crawled through the marshes towards the Iraqi side. He estimated that it took him sixteen hours to crawl through the marshes to reach an area where he would find the Arabs of the marshes.

Extending across the boundaries between Iraq and Iran, the marshes were called the Venice of Iraq. All the inhabitants were Arabic Muslims. The tribes would use specially built narrow long boats called *mashoof*, to transport themselves across the marshes.

As soon as Mohammed saw one of the Arab's houses, he realised he was safe and came out of the water. He received a great and warm welcome from them. They offered him food and drink, not realising the extent of his injuries, but all he wanted was to get to Omara Hospital. The tribal family laid him in a *mashoof* and took him to the nearest road, where he continued his journey by hitchhiking.

I examined his wounds before calling his family. When I removed the dressing to take a look at the wounds I couldn't believe my eyes. The fish hadn't just nibbled on the surface of his skin; they had torn away chunks of his flesh. The erosion on the buttock was deep, down to the muscle, some of which had also been eaten by the fish. Nothing but plastic surgery would be able to help him.

We cleaned the area, dressed it and gave him the usual antibacterial precautions. I told him to stay in Omara and I would ask one of the plastic surgeons to assess him. He refused, as had all the soldiers I had met, all desperately wanting to see their families. I didn't argue with him and told the junior Doctor to put some non-stick dressings on his buttock and give him a medical report before letting him go.

Three months later, Mohammed had plastic surgical repairs on his buttock. He had some complications, but pulled through without any serious problems. During his sick leave he continued coming to help me in the clinic before eventually going back to finish military service. He finished and was released from military service in 1987.

When he was allowed home for good, his wife performed a very big religious ceremony to celebrate his safe return home. He was very happy that he had survived the war. He bought a car for the first time in his life and also managed to buy a piece of land to build his own house. Within a year of his release from the Army he had established himself well within society with his lovely family. He had full-time work in the hospital in the mornings and in my private practice in the afternoons.

On 8th August 1988 it was declared on TV and radio that the war was officially over. The whole country celebrated the end of this vicious, meaningless eight year war. I held a party at my house as my brother Ahmed, who was a Colonel in the Army, had also come home safe and sound. Iraq did not sleep for days as celebrations broke out on the streets of every city. Music blasted out from every street corner and people shot their guns into the air, the traditional and somewhat a paradoxical way to celebrate peace in Iraq.

At 2 a.m. on 9th August 1988 I was called to my local hospital in Hilla. I wasn't on-call but the Doctors in A&E wanted me there. A casualty had been brought in who had been out in his car celebrating when a stray bullet went through his head. When I arrived at the hospital, my heart sank as I saw Mohammed's wife and children huddled around the dead body. I told myself that he had died happy, but the rest of us were left mourning the consequences of such a sick and twisted fate.

CASE EIGHT

I find it extremely difficult to write about this incident, as it is not easy to translate my feelings into words. It was April 1985, springtime in Iraq, lovely weather.

It was my turn to go to Basra, in the south of Iraq, located on Shatt Al-Arab, which was the river made by the uniting of the Euphrates and Tigris in the south of Iraq at a point about 40 Kilometres north of Basra called Al Kurna. The river runs on the eastern border of Basra and finishes at the Arabian Sea, at a point called Alfaw Peninsula. Shatt Al-Arab in its entirety was Iraqi and its furthest bank – the left bank – constituted the official border landmark with Iran.

However, in 1975, Vice President Saddam Hussein met the Shah of Iran in Algeria and they signed a treaty in which Saddam actually agreed to give half of Shatt Al-Arab to Iran. Following that the Iran-Iraq boundary became the deepest point of Shatt Al-Arab, with its left bank becoming Iranian water and the right side remaining Arabic.

This agreement was a concession from Saddam Hussein to the Shah of Iran in return for the latter agreeing to close the northern boundaries between the Kurdish area of Iraq and Iran. Saddam wanted to entrap the Kurds to prevent them from escaping from Iraq into Iran. By putting them under the full control of Saddam Hussein, this made the Kurds very vulnerable.

It was a political treaty that robbed Iraq of its full right to its only waterway into the Arabian Sea. We had no other water boundaries in Iraq. Therefore, following this treaty, there was actually no geographical separation between Basra and the south of Iran. The two nations had long intermingled via marriage and other social relationships.

There was actually a bridge that took you from one side to the other called Al Tennoma. The people in the south of Iran are Arabic in every aspect, especially the cultural part of their lives. They speak Arabic in the two main southern Iranian towns in the area, Abbadan and Al-Muhammara. These areas had the same culture and habits as the people of Basra.

Basra was considered to be the hottest war zone which saw the fiercest fighting. The city was actually a war front. In 1980, soon after the start of the war, the residents of Basra started migrating to the middle lands of Iraq (mainly Babylon) and other southern cities in Iraq. There was not enough accommodation for them and the majority of them lived in war refugee camps.

After a couple of years, Basra was a ghost town with no civilian life, no shops, no restaurants, just an Army. The town's huge and impressive teaching hospital overlooked Shatt Al-Arab. People in vital services for the town like soldiers, security officers, Doctors, and oil and petroleum service workers were not allowed to leave the town. Their families were told to leave without them if they wanted a chance of survival.

When we were assigned to Basra, we spent the whole time in the hospital. When there was no active fighting, and there were no casualties, we often had nice social gatherings; a welcome distraction to the death and destruction surrounding us.

The hospital had a very social environment due to the large number of hospital staff and visiting teams from all over the country. It was a chance for us to meet and swap news, and you would often see a friend whom you had not seen for many years. We sometimes played games such as table tennis, snooker, dominoes, backgammon and chess to pass the time and forget where we really were.

One of the surgeons I saw in Basra was Dr Hussain, who I had already met twelve months before. He was three years senior to me at medical school and had studied and trained for surgery in the United States, gaining his post-graduate American Board in surgery before returning home. Although I knew of him as a senior medical student when we were at medical school in Baghdad, I had not met him socially until 1984, when a close mutual friend of ours arranged a dinner party in Babylon.

Hussain was at the party with his wife and three teenage boys. At that time I had three daughters, the eldest of whom was only five, but our wives seemed to get on very well together. He was a very sociable man with a lovely and likeable personality. He was also great fun, with a very good sense of humour. He was witty, highly educated and a descendent of a middle-class family from the south of Iraq. He seemed to have adopted a very friendly relationship with his teenage children, treating them more like friends; they seemed to openly love and adore him. At the end of the party we exchanged telephone numbers and promised that we would arrange a get together at our house in Hilla.

The next time we actually met was at Al Jumhuri in Basra in 1985. It was a nice surprise and a great opportunity to catch up and socialise; we became very close while we were based there.

One of our favourite times of the day was mealtime. The restaurant was on the second floor and overlooked Shatt Al-Arab, where you could see the military movement on both sides of the river. We would usually have a set menu with the main course of the day being lunch. Abood the cook was a very quiet and friendly chap in his fifties; he was naturally very obliging and did anything you asked him to do. For example, we would ask him to fry rather than boil the chicken, or add in some extra flavour.

One very popular Iraqi dish is called *tashreeb*, which is boiled chicken in its stock, poured on fried bread with chickpeas, eaten without rice. Some of us would ask Abood to serve the chicken for us as *tashreeb*. At about 1 p.m. on that day, I had finished operating on an obstructed umbilical hernia and went up to the restaurant, looking forward to my meal and relaxing with friends. The restaurant was a very large open plan hall and was nearly full by the time I had come up to eat.

Some of the junior Doctors sitting in the corner invited me to join them. I went over and asked Abood to serve my chicken with onions and rice. As I started my lunch, I spotted Dr Hussain coming into the restaurant. He had a quick look around to see if there were any empty seats and then decided to go straight to the kitchen to chat to the cook. As usual, I could see that he was teasing Abood, putting his arm around his shoulder and making jokes, no doubt to get his chicken made into *tashreeb*.

I got up and headed towards the kitchen to chat with them both. As I headed for the kitchen, a deafening bang filled the room and the building shook. The laughter and chatter of the restaurant was fast replaced with bloodcurdling screams of pain and horror. Broken glass from the windows shattered across the room. The dining room looked like a battlefield within seconds; dust, shrapnel, blood and limbs scattered everywhere.

It was difficult to see through the debris and to identify the casualties. Those of us that could, got up onto our feet to assess the situation. I heard women screaming in the kitchen and turned my attention in that direction. I could see Dr Hussain's head rolling on the floor, with slight movement from his lips and eyes. His body laid a few metres away, just outside the kitchen.

A few seconds later and that would have been my head rolling on the floor. A direct, unobstructed missile had come through the kitchen window, amputating Hussain's head, which was then sent rolling into the restaurant. The missile killed Abood and six other Doctors and nurses who were eating at a nearby table. The missile completed its journey by hitting the hard wall at the far end of the dining hall.

One of the casualties was a seven month pregnant gynaecologist who worked at Al Jamhori hospital in Basra. Being a travelling missile, all the injuries were to the head and upper part of the body. The gynaecologist had been hit in the upper part of her chest. I watched in shock as one of her colleagues tried to resuscitate her but she was clearly not going to survive the massive injury she had sustained.

I ran back to the dining hall and stood over Dr Hussain's headless body. My thoughts went immediately to his lovely family, his wife and his children. I imagined them at that very moment eating lunch at their house, talking about when their dad would be home, blissfully unaware of his horrific fate. Ten Doctors and nurses died instantly that day. The incident was never reported by the Iraqi press, their deaths were simply added onto the figure of war casualties for that day.

I don't think that I have ever come to terms with what I witnessed, nor how close I had come to being sent home in a wooden box myself. I often replay that day in my mind, wishing that I had called Dr Hussain over to my table, wishing I could have saved at least one life, that of a dear friend.

CASE NINE

It was around 2 p.m. on a spring day in 1986 and I was about to finish my working day at *Al Jamhori* hospital in Hilla, when the Director gathered all the Doctors together and told us not to leave the hospital because the Mayor was on his way.

We were gathered in a lecture theatre and told to wait there patiently until the Mayor arrived; none of us knew what was going on and stood there with vacant expressions trying to figure out what the Mayor could want so urgently.

Within the hour the Mayor, accompanied by the Head of *Al-Amin* and the *Health Director General* arrived to the lecture hall and took their place on the platform. The Mayor spoke in a very calm and relaxed fashion:

'Thank you all for waiting. I know most of you are dying to rush home to eat or get in your afternoon siesta...but I'm here to share some strictly confidential news with you. I want to make it clear that this is a matter of national security and those who disclose this information will suffer the consequences. I expect you not to share this with your wives when you get home this evening. I think I have made myself understood.' He looked round the room for nods of agreement, the message was loud and clear.

'About three hours ago, an unfortunate accident happened near *Al-Eskandaria*. A truck carrying 'American flour' was passing through the town, when it hit an old railway track and toppled over. The barrels of flour smashed open and covered the streets; children playing nearby grabbed as much of the flour as they could and took it home to their families. It seems that word spread fast, as when officials arrived at the scene, most of the barrels were missing'.

'Doctors, the barrels did not contain flour. They contained sulphur mustard, or as you may know it, mustard gas'. There was a stunned silence in the room. 'We are certain that those illiterate peasants are going to eat the powder, most probably making lovely American bread and cakes.' He laughed in a sickening manner, as if he was enjoying the thought.

'Consequently you are going to receive some very ill patients. Under no circumstances are you to diagnose these symptoms as related to mustard gas poisoning. I do not want to see a single medical report referring to the possibility of mustard gas, is this understood?' Again we all nodded. 'You are to diagnose these patients with food poisoning or food allergies. I hope you realise that we are acting in the interests of our beloved country.'

He then turned to the Head of Al Amin to invite him to comment; he smiled and said 'These are intelligent men; I think the last thing they want is a visit from us.' And with that, they left the room.

The following day, intrigued by the story, I went in my car to the scene of the accident; I stopped nearby and pretended to inspect my tyres. The lorry had been removed but there was a yellow coloured powder covering an area of about fifty square metres on the main road and the sandy hard shoulder. There were tyre marks over the powder; only god knows how far people had carried the mustard gas on their tyres for.

It transpired that the truck was on its way to an industrial plant near *Al Askandaria*; for security reasons, the truck had a huge logo on the side saying, in Arabic 'flour'. The barrels themselves only had English writing on them, so everybody assumed that it was American flour. At that time, the flour in the supermarkets in Iraq was appalling; because of the sanctions and rations, they had been mixing the flour with sand. So to find tonnes of 'American flour' on your doorstep was almost like winning the lottery. Families were cooking with the flour that they had scraped off the streets and had even used the empty barrels to contain drinking water.

For the following days and weeks we saw a massive surge in 'food poisoning', many people became severely ill and disfigured, most of them dying within days. We had our hands tied and could do nothing but watch them suffer; it was heartbreaking to see the extent of the damage to their bodies. I remember a man bringing me his 30 year old wife a couple of years after the incident; she had a severe neurological disorder with near total paralysis. He told me that, since eating the American flour, she had fallen ill and her condition had deteriorated as each day passed. She had also been pregnant at the time and their son was born disfigured and blind. The man didn't understand how the flour had made her react this way.

The government let the Iraqi people believe that it was American owned flour, knowing that it would only fuel people's hatred for the West.

I doubt that any of my colleagues will have told their families about this incident; I didn't tell Mary until we arrived to England in 1990.

DESPERATE TIMES

After the first anniversary of the start of the war, the people of Iraq realised that the war was not going to end in the foreseeable future. They became very worried for their children. To avoid their children being recruited as soldiers, some families tried all that they possibly could to have their sons classified as 'unusable' by making them, in one way or another, disabled.

Unfit soldiers would either be exempt from military service altogether, or, if the disability was not very bad, they would be taken into a non-fighting military job such as a chef or cleaner. Such roles in the Army reduced the risk of being killed. Soldiers that had lost an eye or a limb while on the frontline were actually very happy about it because they knew that they would be able to go back home.

Some soldiers took it to the extreme by inflicting injuries on themselves during their off-duty periods in order to avoid being sent back to the frontline. The desperate young men began thinking up ways to disable themselves that would not be noticed by Saddam and the government.

One popular method was to deliberately cause serious road traffic accidents. When soldiers came home during leave from the Army they started acting aggressively when driving and dealing with others. They would purposefully cause accidents on the streets to try to injure themselves or somebody else so that they would get arrested and not be sent back to the warzone. It was not uncommon to hear about soldiers deliberately hitting pedestrians or other drivers to cause serious damage and in some cases death.

This sort of behaviour was quickly recognised by the government through the Military Information Department, who reported back to Saddam about the soldiers' activities. Saddam issued an order stating that soldiers who caused, or were involved in any form of offence, should be immediately arrested and sent back to their unit. He ordered that these soldiers were to be placed in the most dangerous and high-risk locations as the spear of the attacking force. Any legal proceedings against them were to be postponed until the war was over. This dramatically reduced the personal and road traffic accidents that occurred. However, it wasn't long before the soldiers and their families began to think of other ways to avoid going back into the Army.

A new type of fraud emerged when soldiers started injecting their limbs with kerosene. When you inject petrol into soft tissue the reaction to the injection is horrendously aggressive. At the time the reaction had not been reported in any medical books or journals. Within twenty-four hours the limbs became swollen and necrotic, turning greenish-black and smelling horrific. Doctors in the hospitals were puzzled by the first few presentations. They had never seen such symptoms before.

As Doctors, we began to notice a pattern in the sex, age and profession of the patients: all were young, male soldiers. Of course, the only lifesaving procedure was amputation. If we didn't amputate the infected limb the patient would become very ill due to the absorption of kerosene and the necrotic material from the limb into their circulation. After amputating the limb the patient would be classified as an invalid, ready to be released from the Army. This activity became very popular with soldiers all over the country and Doctors started talking about the prevalence of such incidents. The amputated part would smell of kerosene but nobody knew how it could have possibly reached the human tissue in this way.

One soldier was brought into the hospital, extremely ill and very toxic with the kerosene. He had delayed coming in because he was scared of the amputation and couldn't go through with the consequences of what he had done. His mother told us exactly how it had happened and within minutes the Information Department was informed.

He was interrogated thoroughly and admitted to the self-inflicted injection. He was dragged away by security officers and we never saw him again. Very soon Saddam picked up on this new trend and another order was circulated; this time to all hospitals and specialists, informing them of the ongoing activity of the soldiers and ordering them not to treat such patients. All Doctors were told to contact the local Military Information Department immediately, who would deal with the case.

I fortunately only received one such person in my private practice and I quickly diagnosed it. After confronting the soldier he broke down and admitted that he had given himself the kerosene injection. I couldn't do anything but comply with the order that we had received, knowing that I would suffer a much worse fate if I didn't follow protocol.

As soon as you contacted the Information Department, an army officer would come and take the patient away from the hospital. They would take them into a room and leave them in isolation. They would watch them die in the most horrific manner as the kerosene poisoned their bodies and they suffered a slow, painful death. Once the soldiers had died they would write the word 'coward' on their death certificate to humiliate them and their family. This practice soon stopped when word spread of the agony that suffering soldiers would face and the humiliation and pain they would cause for their family. The soldiers knew that they had to find new ways of injuring themselves to avoid going back to their units.

One evening I was relaxing with my family in our garden, having dinner. The doorbell rang and I went to open the door. There was a very respectable gentleman in his mid-fifties with his wife, two daughters and teenage son. I asked how I could help them. The gentleman started praising my family and our position in society, and started talking about his relationship with my father and uncle. He then came to the point of his visit.

'Sir,' he said, 'I am fifty-eight and my wife is fifty-five. I have one son and two daughters. I have a heart condition and my son is the only future heir. He is my only hope that a man will be looking after the women in the house after my death.

My son, sir, is a soldier at the frontline. He has been nearly killed twice in the last few months. God saved him for us and now he has been with us on leave for only two days and they are calling him back to the frontline.'

I interrupted him and told him how sorry I was for his situation. I then asked in what way I was able to help him.

He got out a large wad of $50 notes, which could easily have been a few thousand pounds. He was trying to pay me to operate on his son. He asked if I could remove his appendix or do a hernia operation on him. When I asked him what his son's symptoms were he told me that he was perfectly fit and healthy, but that they wanted me to remove his appendix to get an official sick note and leave from the army.

I tried to explain my principles as a surgeon. I could not perform any operation if it was not indicated. I tried to speak to him on a level that he understood. I tried to explain about our fate and how if I operated on him when he was fit and well, his son may develop complications from the operation and may die that way.

As I was talking he turned to his wife, stretched out his hand for hers, and asked her for more money. He forced it towards me.

'This is 10,000 Iraqi dinar, Doctor.'

I tried my best not to upset them and to make them understand my principles but I was getting nowhere. They were adamant that their son should have an operation to avoid returning to his unit. Eventually he became very offended, got into his car without saying a word, and before driving away rolled the car window down

'My son will have his operation tonight, Doctor,' he said. 'You will see that there are surgeons around that are much kinder and more sympathetic than you are.'

With anger, he sped away.

The following day I arrived in the hospital car-park and found the man and his wife standing by their car outside the private wing of the government hospital in Babylon. When they saw me driving in they looked the other way to avoid eye contact.

I walked into the hospital and went straight to the patient records to look at the list of patients admitted the night before. There he was. His son had been admitted by another consultant surgeon and operated on at 12 midnight. A normal appendix was removed and the soldier was given sick leave. I wondered how many other surgeons were doing this across the country and how many of these young boys would survive such invasive and unnecessary surgery.

Maybe this sort of practice would be investigated thoroughly in other countries, but not in Iraq; I knew that reporting this incident would only lead to the execution of both the surgeon and the soldier. Some things were better left alone.

Realising the extreme lengths that soldiers were going to, in order to avoid fighting, Saddam decided to legalise a new punishment. An official order was issued, stating that people who tried to avoid fighting in the war should be clearly and visibly marked and identified as cowards. To mark them as such Saddam decided that they should have one ear cut off.

At first nobody took this seriously. That was until the first patient arrived at our hospital in Babylon, escorted by soldiers with a military order to say that his right ear should be cut off. The young boy was taken straight to theatre where he had his ear removed. Saddam made it clear that following this punishment nobody was allowed to cover their deformity. They were forced to go about their daily lives with their visible disfigurement.

These soldiers, besides suffering the mutilation and degrading humiliation, would again be sent off to the most dangerous locations on the war front. Over time the appearance of deformed men across all cities in Iraq was not an uncommon sight.

SADDAM'S DISLIKE OF DOCTOR'S

All the stories about these soldiers had been reported directly back to Saddam through the Military Information Department. Saddam was very well known for his dislike of Doctors for reasons that backdated to his childhood.

Allegedly, when he was nine or ten years old he accompanied his mother to the accident and emergency department at their local hospital. Rumours state that young Saddam would sit idly in the waiting room, dressed in the underprivileged attire that was reflective of his family's wealth. It is said he glared at the prosperous Doctors who were all well dressed, well spoken and clearly socially competent in conversing with nurses and such. Such jealousy fuelled his hatred and so he kept telling his friends and inner circle how Doctors were arrogant, big headed and not to be trusted.

The reports of soldiers wanting to have operations to disable themselves had led the President to be harbour strong suspicions about the trustworthiness of Doctors, especially those serving at the frontier hospitals. He was suspicious that Doctors were becoming more sympathetic to the soldiers than to the tactics pursued by his own regime.

For that reason he requested an independent external audit from a foreign medical organisation to review all the case records of patients operated in the first two-and-a-half years of the war. I heard, but am not really certain, that he got a European medical consultation company to do the audit. Thankfully the results of the audit reflected excellent performance of medical teams with low complication rates.

The results indicated very few Doctors had agreed to perform unnecessary surgery on soldiers and there were very few questionable medical records. The President was impressed and satisfied with the outcome. He ordered the Military Medical Directorate to select a sample of top surgeons and anaesthetists and to submit the names to his office.

The first list, of eight surgeons and anaesthetists, were nominated, and I was one of them. The President asked to meet with us. We were the first of many similar meetings that Saddam requested with front-line Doctors.

At the time I was completely unaware of the audit and had no idea why Saddam Hussein was asking to see me in person. There was no explanation attached to the invite, but I knew that I had been selected along with other Doctors; which was the only slightly comforting factor.

Naturally I was worried and couldn't sleep the night before, running possible scenarios through my mind. I spent the whole night discussing with Mary what I could have said wrong or done to offend the regime. I started to question even the smallest comments or gestures that I had made in the past few weeks and how they could have been misinterpreted.

Mary and I talked about all the possible outcomes of the meeting and we even talked about how she would manage life with our children if I vanished or was killed. Mary was always optimistic, at least on the outside, and convinced me that I had done nothing wrong; with my good reputation behind me I should relax and be confident about meeting with the President.

Time passed slowly but eventually Thursday morning came around and we were told to arrive at Al Rashid Hospital in Baghdad where we would be picked up and driven to the palace. I arrived at the hospital and there were about four or five other Doctors waiting, some I knew by face but none were actually people I knew well. Six were military Doctors who were dressed in their military uniforms, a Kurdish anaesthetist and I.

A famous high-ranking military Doctor, who was the Director General of the Medical Directorate in the Army, escorted us. He was later killed by Saddam himself in a horrific manner; a story which is touched on later on in the book.

We got onto a small, brand new air-conditioned bus and were driven to the palace. The silence amongst us was deafening. I could hear my own heart beating. Some Doctors sitting next to each other would whisper small talk every now and then, most probably trying to distract themselves from where the bus was heading.

As we approached the palace we were instructed on how to behave in the presence of his Excellency. We got off the bus and were ushered into a huge entrance hall; the building was beautiful and graceful. There were smart military guards standing on every corridor and the entrance hall was the most stunning I had ever seen. We were led into a very luxuriously furnished room and were asked to be seated.

About ten minutes later the Chief of Bodyguards, whom we all knew from his appearance on TV, walked in and stood behind a very impressive hand-carved chair. The President followed within seconds.

We stood up and he greeted us in an Arabic way by saying *'alsalamo alaykum shabab'*, meaning 'may peace be upon you young men'. He then went around shaking hands with each one of us. We did not need to introduce ourselves to him as he was addressing us by name. In fact, he not only knew our names but he knew everything about each Doctor in the room.

If one of us had recently lost a relative he consoled that person, if one of us had had a recent addition to the family he would ask about the baby by his or her name. Of course, he knew that by appearing friendly in this way he was also making it clear that there was nothing he didn't know. Saddam was the master of intimidation and this apparently kind gesture instilled fear in us all.

He didn't seem to be pressed for time, as you would expect a President to be. He was calm and relaxed, paying each of us a great deal of attention. This was not a show for the cameras, as there was not one member of the press in the Palace. He sat on an ordinary chair facing us, not at the top of the room where we would usually saw him on TV.

We were served cold soft drinks in beautiful crystal glasses on silver trays, by waiters in black uniforms with white gloves. With a smile on his face he sat back and chatted to us about the Iranians and about their stubbornness during the war. He then spoke highly about our performance as Doctors and thanked us for our medical support, asking us to pass on his thanks to our colleagues. We sat and listened, nodding our heads in agreement to everything he said, regardless of whether we actually agreed or not. This was not a place for freedom of speech.

As he stood up to leave the room, he made his characteristic loud laugh.

'Well, young men, it's not time for dinner yet so I can't invite you to stay. I am sure you all have important commitments to attend to, so I will leave you in peace and may God always be with you'.

He took one or two steps towards the exit of the room and then turned to the Chief of Staff.

'Give the boys their chicks,' he said.

I was with Saddam Hussein in his palace and about to leave with a chick in my hand. It was an odd gesture but I smiled with gratitude. I stood there picturing my family's reaction when I came home with a little chick in my pocket from Saddam; the last present anyone would expect him to give. We saluted him as he left the room and the Chief of Staff asked one of the low-ranking officers standing near him to bring us our keys to the chicks. Keys? Why did we require keys? I could sense the tension and panic in the room, we all knew the sort of sadistic games that Saddam could play. I began to wonder whether this was a euphemism for something much more sinister.

Five minutes later, a military officer walked into the room. He held a tray in his hand, on which were a pile of black keys. Each key carried on it the Mercedes logo. He brought the tray round to each one of us, asking us to pick a key. There was a plastic tag attached to each one with a number written on it. After each one of us picked a key, in silence, the Chief of Staff asked us to follow him out of the waiting room.

After a short walk through the palace we reached a huge parking area where hundreds of brand new untouched 190 Mercedes were parked meticulously in covered garages. Saddam would notoriously call the 190s "chicks", as they were the smallest Mercedes of the time.

'Gentlemen,' the Chief said, 'here are your chicks. Your keys are attached to a tag that carries the number of your car, and I hope you find it easily. Have a safe journey home'.

I was escorted by a soldier to my allocated vehicle and drove out of Saddam's Palace in my brand new Mercedes. As I was driving home, I began wishing that he had offered us chickens; maybe I would have ended up with an AMG!

SADDAM AND I

I had expected that to be the first and last time that I would meet Saddam Hussein. I was completely unaware that that would be the first of many times that Saddam would enter my life.

Saddam affected the lives of the Iraqi people, including my own family, and myself in many different ways. There were many members of my own family and close friends who were unfortunate enough to experience the cruel and sadistic ways of Saddam as a dictator.

However, it would not be fair nor accurate if I did not also recall the times that he personally helped me, my friends and my family when needed. For that reason I have divided the anecdotes of this chapter into the good, the bad and the ugly.

All but one of the following events happened whilst I was living in Iraq between 1978 and 1990. These were not my only experiences with Saddam and his circle, but I believe that they provide insights into the world that we were forced to live in.

THE GOOD

My British Friend

When I first went to England in 1971 to study surgery I was based at New Cross Hospital in Wolverhampton with many other foreign Doctors and nurses. At the time I had met a very likeable Egyptian Doctor who had studied medicine in Cairo and was training to be an orthopaedic surgeon. He was going out with a physiotherapist, Gillian, who was a very nice girl, full of life and fun.

She was very talkative, had a very good sense of humour and she seemed to like the Arabs, in particular the Iraqis. She would try to pick up Arabic words and learn more about the culture. Gillian seemed to develop respect for me as I was generally quieter than my friends. Although I liked going out, I would not make a fool of myself and would remain respectful to everybody. Her relationship with the orthopaedic trainee was very hectic and unstable. I knew very well that their relationship would not last.

There was also another Iraqi Doctor with us who was training to be a psychiatrist. Doctor Adel was quite unpopular and none of us really liked him. He never managed to make friends and had loads of girls on the go at the same time. His presence was heavy and unpleasant. He wasn't easy to get on with and had no sense of humour at all.

Gillian slowly started to feel sorry for him and pay him more attention; at every party she would speak to him to make sure that he wasn't left out. Before long she had finished her relationship with the Egyptian trainee and started dating Doctor Adel. By this point my time at New Cross Hospital had come to an end and I moved on for further training in other parts of the UK. I never saw any one of the 'gang' again.

9 Years later

At about 8 p.m. on a pleasant evening in April 1981, ten months after the war started, I was sitting in our house in Hilla. My little daughter May was playing around Mary who was pregnant with Hannah, our second daughter. The telephone rang and a man introduced himself as the receptionist at Al Salam Hotel in the Al-Karrada Province of Baghdad.

'I have with me,' he said, 'an English lady, who I am sorry to say is currently in her nightwear beside me. She is very distressed and asking for help. She claims that her husband threw her out of the house and she doesn't have anybody that she knows in Iraq except for a Doctor from the Bhayah family. We managed to speak to one of your cousins, Majhid Bhayah, who lives nearby and as soon as we mentioned your name he gave us your telephone number in Babylon.'

He told me that they had given her a jacket to cover herself and made her a cup of tea and something to eat. I asked him to pass the telephone onto the girl so that I could speak with her directly. As soon as she got on the phone she was distressed and crying.

'Please Doctor Ismaiel, help me,' she started. 'I don't know if you remember me. My name is Gillian and we were at New Cross Hospital together in Wolverhampton. I have been living in Baghdad and my husband has beaten me up and thrown me out of the house in my nightwear. I don't have a penny in my pocket and I don't know anyone else in the whole country. I ran across the road, straight to this hotel, to ask for help and see if I could sleep here for the night. They have taken good care of me but I really need your help.'

Of course I remembered her and knew full well who her husband was. I was angry and disgusted about how ill-mannered he had been. In Iraq, whatever happens with you and your family, in particular with your wife, you should not let her out onto the streets as she is your honour and your respect.

'Gillian,' I said, addressing her by her first name. 'Please do not tell me that you are married to Doctor Adel.'

She began crying down the phone and told me that she had moved to Iraq with him after they got married, and was currently living with his mum and mentally disabled sister in the same house. They treated her very badly and were beating her regularly.

I explained to her that I lived over a hundred kilometres away from Baghdad and asked her if she wanted to come straight to us or would she prefer to stay the night at the hotel and I would arrange for her to come to us the following morning. She jumped at the chance to come straight to our house, saying that she needed to get away from her husband because she was scared.

I told the hotel receptionist to book her a taxi and to tell them that I would pay the driver on her safe arrival to Babylon. I got off the phone and told Mary the whole story, so she started preparing the guest room for Gillian and some refreshments for her arrival.

At about midnight a taxi pulled up outside my house in Babylon. Gillian stepped out, looking withdrawn and exhausted. Mary was with me at the door to greet her and I introduced them to each other, paid the taxi driver and thanked him for his help. The moment Gillian walked into the house, Mary offered her a shower, gave her some fresh towels, some clothes and new pyjamas. She showed her to the guest room where Gillian managed to get a comfortable night's sleep. It was in the early hours of the morning and we didn't want to exhaust her any more by finding out all the details of her situation, but Mary and I sat up most of the night discussing how her husband could have done this to her.

The following morning we all had breakfast together and I left the two women to chat while I went to work. I suspected that Gillian would be more comfortable explaining the story to Mary and that I would hear it from Mary when I got home.

It transpired that as soon as Doctor Adel had got Gillian to Iraq, he started treating her badly and would physically beat her on a daily basis. His mum and mentally retarded sister, whom she spent all day taking care of, would give her total hell. They used her as a slave to clean and cook and she wasn't allowed breaks or time off. She became a full time carer for his sister, feeding, bathing and changing her every day.

It was not the life that he had promised her when they got married and she asked him for a divorce because she could not deal with the way that she was being treated. It turned out that Doctor Adel outright refused and said that he would never let her return to the UK. He confiscated her passport and all her belongings and locked them away. She was never allowed out alone and he would never give her money to spend on herself or on the house.

When I heard the story from Mary, I decided to contact Doctor Adel to try to reason with him and tell him that if he didn't love her and didn't want to treat her with respect he should let her go and give her the passport back. I expressed my disappointment about him treating a foreign lady in this manner, especially when he knew full well that she had no family or friends to turn to, to resolve their problem.

He refused to compromise and hung up the phone in my face. I decided to contact his elder brother and mutual friends, to ask them to intervene and try to reason with him. I rang them and explained my concerns.

They were all supportive and sympathetic with his wife and agreed that we should meet at my house for dinner. I invited her husband to my house in the hope that between us all we could give Gillian her freedom back. In Iraq, most conflicts would be resolved in this way, so Mary cooked everybody a lovely dinner and we sat down and began to discuss how to resolve the problem. I explained that we did not want to intrude on their lives but that Gillian was a friend and we wanted to help her. Everybody around the table agreed that he was not treating her the way that he should and that if their problems were so bad, he should grant her a divorce and let her return to the UK.

Doctor Adel was a very obnoxious and arrogant man. He refused to take her to Baghdad and refused to give her the passport back. He stood up half-way through the meal and left my house, leaving Gillian behind. I tried to shout to him to stop and to listen to us.

'Doctor Adel,' I said, 'you are not helping yourself here. If you leave my house without solving this I will take matters further and that will definitely not be in your favour. I may not be a powerful man, but I know many men that are and I will find a way for Gillian to get her passport back.'

In a very spiteful way he told me that I could do whatever I liked and that his wife would not be allowed to go back to England. Everybody left my house and Mary, Gillian and I felt that we were back to square one. She kept apologising over and over for troubling us and explained that she wouldn't have contacted me if she hadn't been so desperate. Both Mary and I sympathised greatly with her and knew that if we did not help her nobody would.

Instead of messing around for months trying to get Doctor Adel to come to his senses, I decided to write to President Saddam Hussein. I knew that he would not accept any woman, whether Iraqi or foreign, to be treated this way in his country. I sat down and drafted a letter to him, explaining the problem very briefly and touching on the shame that would be brought to the country if we left this lady in the hands of her cruel husband.

I asked for his help to get her passport back safely and to grant her a divorce to allow her to return back to England. I posted the letter into one of the post-boxes specifically assigned for the President that were placed at different sites across Baghdad. Letters left in these post boxes did not require stamps; they simply had to be addressed for the attention of His Excellency.

Within forty-eight hours I received a phone call from Al-Amin in Baghdad, the most feared government department. Everybody knew that if you were taken in by Al-Amin you would never come out alive. I had heard of the most horrific tortures happening there, including throwing people into nitric acid baths while they were alive. Getting involved or being imprisoned by them was the worst nightmare an Iraqi could have.

When I realised who was on the other line, I spoke with great hesitation.

'I am calling in reference to your letter to the President,' the officer said. 'Is the English lady still with you, sir?'

'Yes,' I answered.

'Can you bring her to our department or do you want us to arrange for her to be picked up from your house tomorrow morning?'

I quickly chose the latter, not wanting to set foot in Al-Amin Headquarters. The next day a white 4x4 arrived at my house and took Gillian to Baghdad. She arrived at the Al-Amin building at 9.30am and was taken straight to a luxuri-

The Hanging Gardens of Babylon

ous office where she was welcomed and offered breakfast. She explained her story about her husband to the officer.

'Well, Madame, following Doctor Bhayah's letter, the President has ordered that your request be granted. He has said that you are our guest in Iraq and that he does not accept that you have been treated in this way. He has told me to personally apologise on behalf of all the Iraqis and assure you that your husband is not an example of a good Iraqi person.'

The man asked Gillian what it would take to make her happy and to fix this mess.

'Just my passport, Sir,' she replied. 'My passport and a one way ticket to England.'

'Fine,' he said, 'wait here one moment please.'

He called a soldier into the room and said, 'Bring the bastard here.'

Within a few seconds her husband was dragged into the room, held from each arm by soldiers, who were both very tall and heavy men. Gillian said that her husband looked pale, shocked and worn. He never said a word or raised his eyes to look at her. The Officer began talking to him.

'People like you bring shame upon us. People like you bring the Iraqis a bad name. You don't seem to have any manners, honour or principles in life. Your colleague, Doctor Bhayah, did all he possibly could to give you a chance to resolve your problem with your wife privately, but you were both stupid and stubborn'.

Still her husband gazed at the floor in silence while the officer continued his rant.

'You have exactly thirty minutes to go to your house, get your wife's passport and £4,000 sterling from the bank to give to her. Do you understand me, or would you like me to explain this to you in a different way?'

Her husband nodded feebly.

'I will do everything you have asked me to do, but please promise to let me go afterwards.'

The officer ignored him and ushered him out of the room. Dr Adel did as he was told and returned to Al-Amin with her passport, a fully packed suitcase of her belongings and £4,000 in English money.

The following day Gillian was granted a legal divorce from her husband in the Civil Court and she used the £4,000 to buy her one-way ticket to England. On that Friday we gave an ecstatic Gillian a lift to the airport.

I later wrote a letter of thanks to Saddam for saving Gillian from the clutches of Doctor Adel. None of us ever found out what happened to her husband at the hands of Al-Amin, but we never heard of him again.

Our Fourth Child

In 1983, Mary was pregnant with our fourth child. Marwan had been taken from us in 1979, but since then we had our two beautiful daughters: May, born in 1979 and Hannah, born in 1981. When Mary was pregnant with Marwan she developed very bad deep vein thrombosis.

The Doctors had warned her that she needed to be careful with each pregnancy and they recommended the use of injections to thin the blood and minimise the chances of a recurrent clot. The drug Heparin was used to minimise the chances of deep vein thrombosis and the possibility of a clot going to the lung, which would have caused a pulmonary embolism. When Mary had been pregnant with both May and Hannah in Iraq she was fully covered with Heparin, even though an ultrasound of her calves showed that she had no clots.

Mary had gone back to England in 1983, as she would do every summer, to see her family. Of course, she took the children with her.

The law in Iraq was that a husband and wife could not leave the country together at the same time. Saddam feared that if a couple were to go abroad they may never come back.

This was enforced most strictly during the war, especially on those who Saddam believed to be valuable, such as Doctors, soldiers and engineers.

While Mary was in England with May and Hannah, my name was once again automatically put on the government travel ban. This was a list of names that would appear at every airport, travel office and border checkpoint of Iraq. We had accepted this as a fact of life. While she was with her family in England, Mary called me and said that her gynaecologist had done an ultrasound of her calves and this had shown a blood clot in her leg. He advised her strongly not to travel on an aeroplane back to Iraq and to start using the Heparin injections. This was just ten days before she was due to fly back home. Mary didn't want to deliver the baby without me being there; I had been by her side when each of the children was born.

It was the 10th August when I was on the phone with Mary discussing our options. She was adamant that she wanted to fly and would accept any risks. She was desperate for me to be with her, whatever it took. I tried to explain to her what she already knew; that the medical care in Iraqi hospitals during the war was not brilliant. I worried about her and advised her to stay there and to have the baby in the UK because it was safer. We ended the call as it was late and decided to talk the following day, to give us both a chance to think straight.

The next day, the Mayor of Babylon asked to see me. This was not unusual; I had regular contact with the Mayor. So, I finished my private clinic and went straight to his office. When I arrived, I found the Chief of Police and Head of Al-Amin also waiting for me at his office. The Leader of the Ba'ath Party in Babylon also arrived once I had got there. I immediately began to panic and wondered what I was needed for. After some pointless chitchat, the Mayor asked me how the madam was. Of course, he was referring to Mary. I told him that I was worried due to her situation and wished that I could be with her when she had the baby.

'Tell the Madam not to come back,' the Mayor said with great confidence.

He wrote down on a piece of paper a four digit telephone number and told me to dial it. I had never seen a four or five digit telephone number in Iraq; there wasn't even an area code.

'His Excellency's direct line, Sir,' he explained.

Instead of feeling happy, apprehension and panic swept over me. I immediately knew that my phone call with Mary had been tapped, as there was only one way they could have known about my situation. I didn't want to call Saddam directly. He was the President and taking full responsibility of his nation at war. What would he have to say to somebody going through such a small and domestic matter?

I decided not to call him straight away, to give myself time to think about what I would say and whether or not I had said anything to offend him during my phone call with Mary. I got home just after 10pm and summoned the courage to dial the number. It had not rung once before somebody picked up on the phone.

'Good evening, Doctor,' the man replied, sounding like an authoritative official. He had clearly been expecting me.

I began to apologise for disturbing him when he interrupted.

'Doctor, please be at the Republican Palace at 4 p.m. tomorrow.'

Before I could even agree he said, 'See you then, have a good night's sleep.' and put the phone down. In spite of his wishes for my good night's sleep I didn't sleep at all that night. A million things went through my mind as I paced around the house, knowing that I had no choice but to go to the palace and accept my fate. I went out to the garden, walking in circles, I simply couldn't settle.

Our Sri Lankan housemaid kept asking if I wanted anything and walked in circles behind me in the garden. She was an absolutely superb housemaid, she always wanted to make sure that we were all okay before she went to bed herself. She also didn't sleep that night, seeing that I was uneasy.

I felt like telling her the whole story, I just wanted to talk to somebody. Unfortunately Kankhanam did not speak much Arabic or English, she was barely able to make herself understood to Mary.

I didn't want to ring Mary, to worry her unnecessarily when she was so close to her delivery date. When morning came round, I went straight to the hospital and didn't say a word to anybody. I didn't eat, I didn't drink, I didn't stop once but to inform my secretary to cancel my afternoon clinic. At 1 p.m. I got into my car and set off for Baghdad.

At the entrance to Baghdad, there was a military checkpoint called Al Dowra. This was one of many checkpoints around the city where you were normally stopped to verify your ID and maybe have your car searched. I was stopped at

Al Dowra by a soldier who indicated for me to pull over. He came towards the car and spoke to me in a very polite voice.

'Dr Ismaiel Bhayah?'

I nodded and said, 'Yes'.

'Would you mind, Sir, getting out of your car and giving me the keys.'

I did as I was told and gave him the keys to my car. He then shouted over to another soldier.

'Can you take the Doctor?'

The other soldier jumped into a grey Range Rover and drove towards me. I got into the air conditioned car and left my 280S Mercedes with the other man. Luckily I had no valuables or weapons inside my car. The chauffer in the grey Range Rover never opened his mouth, and neither did I. I didn't ask where we were going or why I had to leave my car behind.

Half an hour's drive later and I recognised the impressive building of the Republican Palace. The road leading up to it was heavily guarded, but the driver was not stopped by any of the guards. He headed for the entrance and stopped outside a small building, which was clearly signposted as the reception area. He got out of the car and opened the door for me. He then led me into a large waiting area where at least a couple of hundred other people were sitting in silence. I went up to the reception desk and the receptionist took me by real surprise when she greeted me.

'Welcome Doctor Bhayah, would you like something to drink?'

'No,' I said. 'But thank you very much for the offer'.

The Hanging Gardens of Babylon

A man dressed in a military uniform, but without a rank on his shoulder, asked me to follow him. He led me to a white 280S Mercedes, but it was not mine. This one had a black curtain at the back and a very long aerial sticking out of its hood, which was not allowed on civilian cars. He drove me in this car for about one kilometre into a 'land of heaven'.

The design of the roads, the gardens, the plants, the flowers, the trees, the turf, were all exquisite. I had never seen a landscape so immaculate, so clean and so perfect. He must have had gardener's working day in, day out, picking up any leaf that fell to the ground and sweeping away any dust from the pathways. It looked like something out of a Disney movie. It was certainly not a landscape that other Iraqis had the luxury of viewing in their own day-to-day lives.

We arrived at another hugely imposing building, which had massive marble pillars and a wide, curved staircase leading up to a huge wooden door. The entrance was so beautiful it gave you a feeling that you were dreaming. I had never understood what people meant when they said they were having an out-of-body experience. Not until that very moment.

As I walked up the steps, I checked the time; it was 2.40 p.m. The entrance hall looked like a church: it had a beautifully hand-carved high dome and paintings covered the walls. The impressive marble floor was lined with tall, hand-crafted stone pillars. Waiters dressed in red and black uniforms and white gloves attended to everybody's needs, offering chilled drinks. I was offered some orange juice, and the moment I had finished my drink a man approached me.

'Doctor,' he said, 'would you mind coming with me this way?'

I followed him and he advised me to take off every single piece of metal I was carrying or wearing. My watch, my ring, my wallet, my belt, my keys and change were taken out and put in an envelope with my name on it. He then asked me to pass through the security arch, and when no alarms went off he guided me into another superb hall. I was so taken aback by the beauty of this place that I had completely forgotten why I was there in the first place.

In this hall, there were rows of desks with officers sat behind them. I was directed to one of the officers and the man addressed me as though he knew me. He asked me if I had any close family who had died as a martyr during the war. He then asked me if I had any close family that had been executed or imprisoned because he was a traitor against the government. Finally he asked me whether I had any first blood relatives living abroad. I answered no to all three questions and he leaned back, and looked up at me.

'Then what relation are you to Imad and Alae Bhayah in Stockholm?'

I had completely forgotten about my first cousins Imad and Ali who had left Iraq to live in Sweden over twenty years ago. I apologised for my mistake and explained that I had forgotten about them because we barely spoke.

'Do you know who they are married to in Sweden?' he asked.

I was trying to remember if they were even married but before I could put an answer together he realised that I was getting nervous because I really didn't know anything.

'Don't worry Doctor, we have the highest respect for you and your family. I just wanted to chat to you about Imad. We went to school together'.

I breathed a sigh of relief, then he pushed a piece of A4 paper and a pen towards me.

'Can you please, Sir, write a very brief note as to why you want to see His Excellency the President.'

He made it very clear that I shouldn't write more than a few lines, so I wrote the following two sentences: 'My wife has a high-risk pregnancy and is currently abroad, due to her health problems I would like to be with her when she delivers our baby. The Mayor of Babylon instructed me to call His Excellency and I was ordered to come here'.

The officer watched over my shoulder as I wrote and then took the piece of paper away from me.

A soldier ushered me into the next room. I had not been prepared for what was about to happen. Saddam had set up a series of rigorous medical tests that had to be passed in order to gain access into the main palace.

At the first station, a dermatologist checked my face, my hands, my fingers and my nails. He could not diagnose any skin diseases and let me pass through. I was then ushered towards a dentist, who checked and x-rayed my teeth to make sure that there were no hidden devices in my mouth. When he was satisfied with his findings I was sent through to a radiologist, who scanned my body for hidden devices, to check that

I wasn't carrying anything dangerous. At the final station an ENT Surgeon checked my ears, nose and throat.

The entire process must not have taken more than fifteen minutes; the efficient organisation of the stations was actually admirable. I was not alone; about twenty other people were going through the same process at the same time. When the medical screening was over we were respectfully led through to the exit of the rounded hall and went through an elegantly designed white corridor.

Along the fifty metre long corridor stood statue-like Republican Guards; they were all tall, well-built and holding a spear in their hands. I didn't see one blink an eye. I had a very odd feeling as I walked through the palace; a deep fear mixed with innate curiosity. I wondered what had happened inside this palace; if the walls could only talk.

At the end of the corridor our guide stopped and turned to us.

'Ladies and gentlemen,' he said, 'you may now be on your way to see the President in person, or you may be directed to see somebody deputised on his behalf. Those of you who are to see the President have to observe the following: don't speak until you are spoken to; don't put your hands in your pocket; don't cross your arms in front of or behind your body, keep your arms straight at your side and do not make a fist; stand distant from the President unless he asks you to approach him; when you are asked a question be brief and concise in your response.'

He then led us into a big office that easily seated all of us. At the top of the room was a huge wooden desk, behind which was a captain whose face was very familiar. I remembered I had seen him on TV standing behind the President. He was one of his closest bodyguards.

We all sat down and Arabic coffee and cold drinks were offered. The captain started picking from a pile of files in front of him. One at a time, he scanned the letters and started calling out names. Almost everyone in the room had been called through and directed to go see one of Saddam's advisors.

Eventually there was only one woman and I left in the room. The captain looked at the last two files in front of him and raised his eyes towards me. He looked at me without saying anything and then turned to a soldier standing next to him.

'Take the Doctor through.'

He took my file in his hand and I followed him into a room attached to the one that we had been sitting in. Each room had been more impressive than the one before it. He asked me to sit down and stood over me.

I felt numb. The reality of my situation had returned to me and I realised that I still did not really know why I was there. I suddenly felt deep regret that I hadn't told Mary that I was coming to see Saddam. If I didn't leave the room alive she would suffer, never knowing what had happened to me. It suddenly dawned on me that not one person actually knew where I was.

Before I had time to panic, the door at the far end of the room opened and out of it appeared the Chief of Staff for President Saddam Hussein, Mr Yaseen. He looked straight at me and I stood up and followed him through the door that he had just come out of.

Dragging my heavy feet I walked into the next room, to find myself face to face with the President. He was tall and nice-looking, with pale skin and very sharp chestnut-coloured eyes like an eagle. He oozed authority. He stood next to his ivory white desk in his military uniform and reading glasses. He had never worn glasses on TV or for public appearances. I guessed that he did not want to be seen as having any weaknesses. As I walked in he removed his reading glasses and put his hand forward towards me, so I stepped forward and was given a very warm welcome.

'How are you, Doctor? How was your journey from Hilla? Did my men treat you well?'

As I was about to answer, he sat behind his desk and asked me to sit on the beautiful leather seat opposite him. He looked at me with a surprisingly kind smile.

'How is your family, Doctor Ismaiel?'

I started to open my mouth to respond, but I was totally speechless. I needed to find a response that was both impressive and concise, but I couldn't believe that I was alone with him, having a private conversation. There was not one other person in the room, just the President and I. But the charming man in front of me did not seem the evil dictator I had regularly heard stories about.

So I calmed my nerves, collected my thoughts and thanked him for asking.

'If you are well Sir then all the Iraqis are,' I said.

'Tell me Doctor Ismaiel, is the Madam going to bring you a baby boy, a brother for your daughters and an heir to the Bhayah Empire? I know that you have very lovely daughters,

I adore mine, but every Arabic man needs a son to carry his name.'

He then paused and waited for me to say something.

'Well Sir,' I said, 'as long as my wife has a safe and sound delivery and the baby is healthy we shall thank God for that, but yes, both Mary and I wish for a baby boy.'

'Well, I think you should be with your wife at this difficult time. If she is exposed to any minute risk we should not allow her to be by herself. You need to go and be with her in England.'

'Sir,' I uttered, lost for words. 'The country is at war and you are a very busy man, I did not come here to waste your time on such a trivial matter.'

'No, no, no,' he shook his finger at me, in a very authoritative manner, a characteristic movement for him. 'Your wife is our guest in this country and we want her to be safe, comfortable and happy. You have to be with her. She is Irish isn't she?'

'Yes, Sir,' I said.

'I like the Irish,' he responded, 'They are warm and friendly people. They are very family orientated. How old are your in-laws Doctor Ismaiel?'

'Mary's mother is old, around sixty, sir'.

Before I went any further, he laughed at me.

'Sixty or even seventy, Doctor Ismaiel, is still a young age in England. They like to enjoy their lives, not like us wrapped in black and sitting in the house waiting to get old. Take your mother-in-law some nice presents; I suggest you take her some heavy, gold Arabic jewellery. You are well off Doctor and I am sure you can afford it. You have to make sure you take respectful presents to your in-laws.'

I nodded and agreed that I would.

'For her father,' he carried on, 'I have seen in the government central supermarket some beautiful Longine and Omega watches, so take your father-in-law one of those'.

I thanked him for his concern and kindness, but he carried on.

'Take enough money to treat them well, life in England is pretty costly.'

He laughed in his characteristic and unique way, with his shoulders going up and down.

'Well, it will be nice for you to have some rain and cool, cold weather in August. I am sure that's how the weather will be in London. I will leave you in peace and wish you a safe journey to England. Please give my regards to your wife and kisses to your daughters.'

As he stood up to leave the room he once again said he wished Mary a safe delivery and hoped that we would have a son. He put his hand forward to shake mine, and I felt honesty, warmth and sincerity from the way he squeezed my hand. I retreated backwards a few steps, not wanting to turn my back to him, and then I left the room. Immediately outside the door, I found the Chief of Staff, Mr Yaseen, waiting in the next room.

Mr Yaseen smiled at me and wished me a safe journey back to Babylon. I was led out of a side door at the end of a very short corridor, when the door opened my white Mercedes was parked waiting for me. The keys were in the ignition and my car had been professionally washed and valeted. I didn't know whether it was an act of kindness or whether it was to disguise a thorough search of my car.

I was escorted off the premises and left the palace in a very happy mood. It had been a while since I had felt that level of happiness, not only because I had met the legendary President Saddam Hussein completely alone and had survived, but also because I was going to be with my wife and daughters.

When I got back to Hilla I went straight to my father's house to tell him about my experience. He listened with great interest and enthusiasm, and asked me about every single detail of our meeting. From his house I rang Mary in England and she was over the moon to hear the story. She was worried that the paperwork to leave was going to take a long time and that I would miss the delivery, but still happy that I was heading over to be with her. I left my father's house to go home and pack.

When I got there Kankhanam, our Sri Lankan housemaid, was in a real state of panic. With the little English language that she spoke, I understood from her that policemen had been looking for me. She was worried and was trying to ask me if I was okay or if I was in trouble.

While she was talking to me in the garden, a white Fiat Argenta arrived at our house with two officers in it. They were from the Passport Office and asked me if I had my passport to hand. They told me that they had received orders from the President's Office to facilitate an exit visa. I told them that it was late and I was tired, but they pleaded with me to allow them to fulfil their order.

I gave them my passport and they asked me to wait for five minutes while they stamped all the necessary pages of my passport and signed the exit visa for me. As soon as they had done it they appeared relieved. It was clear that they needed to report back to their boss that night, to be allowed to go home. That sort of paperwork would have taken me weeks to complete. Yet within five minutes of arriving home my passport had been stamped and I was ready to leave the country.

I went into the house to pack, and the phone rang. It was the Minister of Health, Doctor Alwash. He was originally from my town, Hilla, and he knew my family very well.

'Good evening, Doctor,' he said, 'where have you been? I have been trying to ring you since 7 p.m.'.

'Well Dr Alwash, I was with His Excellency the President.'

I felt pride and defiance saying this, because I had already applied for a two week holiday before Mary left. The Minister had refused it without giving a valid reason, for which I didn't like him. Now I knew he was chasing me to give me my holiday before he retired to bed.

'Yes, I know, Ismaiel,' he said. 'I have ordered your Managing Director to give you open-ended leave with full salary.'

I thanked him and told him that I would call first thing in the morning to the Managing Director's office to get it. Dr Alwash immediately panicked.

'No, no, no, you have to go and get it now. I have to report back to the President's office tonight that I have done what I was ordered to do'.

I explained that I was too exhausted to go and pick it up, deep down wanting him to feel the misery that he had put me through only a few weeks before by refusing my annual leave application. Eventually he pleaded with me to stay awake so that he could send the written declaration of leave directly to my house. I agreed to this and waited for its arrival.

I slept well that night, happy and contented. At 6 a.m. the phone in the bedroom woke me up, this time it was my eldest brother Ibrahim, who was the Managing Director of Rafidyn Bank in Babylon.

'Good morning,' he said. 'Where the hell were you last night? I was ringing your house until 10pm and then I gave up'

'Why?' I asked, 'what's the problem?'

'Problem?' he said. 'I wish it was a problem. It would have been much easier to deal with. The President's office has given me instructions to change travellers' cheques for you to the amount of £10,000 English pounds. Do you realise that the official allowance is only £250? Can you please put my mind at rest and tell me exactly why the President's office is telling me to give my brother thousands of pounds in travellers' cheques to go abroad? In fact, you need to come to the bank and exchange your money so that I can report back immediately, so you can tell me when you get here.'

He sighed and hung up. I went down to the bank to pick up my money and then we went for lunch with the rest of my family, where I filled everyone in on my story.

Within less than twelve hours of visiting the President I had achieved the impossible. I was given permission to leave the country, I had my paperwork approved, my passport stamped, was given sixty days leave with full salary and £10,000 in travel money. Once I had everything I needed, I rang Mary to give her the good news, got changed and went to the hospital. When I arrived, as usual, I called in to the Director's office to say good morning and have a cup of tea before going to do a ward round.

'What are you doing here Ismaiel?' the Director asked, as he ushered me into his office and shut the door behind us.

'I am coming in to do a round and then I have clinic,' I said.

'No clinic, no patients, no ward round. Your colleagues will do that. You are on holiday from today for sixty days and if they find out I made you work it will cost me more than my job. I don't want to know now Ismaiel, but some day you will have to tell me the story about how exactly you got Saddam Hussein to do all of this for you.'

I left the hospital, not wanting to cause trouble for him.

I went to the Iraqi Airline office in Hilla and told them I needed a ticket to England. The director of the airline was a family friend and told me that all of the aeroplanes to England were fully booked for the next two months. He told me that the earliest date I could leave was early October. I appealed to him to contact the Head Office and check if there had been any cancellations. I didn't want to tell him the entire story straight away, but I knew that if I got stuck I would tell him everything.

He agreed to ring the Head Office, but there wasn't a single available seat with it being holiday season. Towards the end of the conversation the man on the other end of the phone asked if he was looking for a ticket for Ismaiel Bhayah of Babylon.

My friend said yes, and asked how he knew. He was told that didn't matter, but just to ask me to name the date and time that I wanted to travel and they would get me on a plane.

I was booked on a flight out of Iraq on the following day. At the airport I was treated like a VIP, I was taken into the first class lounge without even checking in. At no point did I go through a security check or baggage inspection. On the plane, I reflected on the last two days. Everything had happened so fast I hadn't stopped to think.

How had Saddam cascaded such information across the government authorities so quickly? And why was he worried about my personal problems? To those questions, I would never know the answers.

I arrived at my in-laws with exactly the gifts that the President had suggested to me. Mary and I had not been abroad together since Marwan's death in 1979, so I spent all the travellers' cheques spoiling my lovely girls.

At 9 p.m. on 20th September 1983 we had a lovely, healthy baby girl. We called our third daughter Nadia.

After a few weeks, when we got back to Iraq, Mary kept telling me to write a short note to thank the President for what he had done for us. She said that he should know that I had not abused his trust and had returned to Iraq within a short time period, rather than staying the entire sixty days. I told her it was absurd to disturb him with such a note. I had met him over a month ago and he was the President of Iraq, not the local Mayor. Mary reluctantly accepted my decision and we continued life as normal, with our newborn baby girl.

A few days later I returned to work and went up to the third floor where my office and surgical unit were located. An envelope had been left on my desk for me. It was marked with the stamp of the President's office. The note read: 'Welcome back Doctor. Congratulations on the birth of your third baby girl, Nadia. God bless you all.' It was signed Saddam Hussein. I wasn't sure what to make of the note. Although it was surely partly intended in kindness, it was also yet another gentle reminder that he was monitoring our every move.

My Dream Hospital

About thirty miles south of Baghdad, on the way to Babylon, there was a very large piece of fertile land through which passed a branch of the Euphrates. It was called the Mussayeb Plant, and it was a great agricultural area and an excellent habitat for birds and wildlife. It was very popular with keen hunters. However, after Saddam came into power he branded it as a VIP shooting range for top government officials only.

One day, whilst I was at my private clinic, I received a series of phone calls. The first was from the Chief of Al-Amin, swiftly followed by a call from the Mayor's office, and then a third from the Managing Director of the Babylon Health Service. All asked me to go immediately to the hospital.

My clinic was heaving that day, people had come from all over Iraq to see me and some had travelled for hundreds of miles to get to my clinic. They would usually turn up without making an appointment and queue outside, being seen by me on a first come, first served basis. That afternoon I had over thirty patients waiting to see me and I had to turn them down without being able to provide a reasonable explanation.

The Hanging Gardens of Babylon

As I was coming down the stairs from the first floor where my private clinic was located, I bumped into a captain from Al-Amin who said that the Director of Al-Amin had sent him to pick me up and take me straight to the hospital. I left my car in the car park and went with the captain, the tyres screeching on the tarmac as he set off at high speed.

I asked the captain what had happened and he told me that he genuinely had no idea. All he had been told was that an urgent call had been received from the palace and that it was related to a member of the President's family being injured at the Mussayeb Plant.

I kept quiet until we arrived at Al Jamhori hospital. Armed military security guards had surrounded the entire hospital and secured all exits. There were over twenty government cars outside; military, police, security and those of the Ba'ath Party leaders in Babylon.

I walked into the building and up to the first floor to find hundreds of military personnel lining the corridors. I went into the Director's room, in which was sat with the Mayor, the Chief of Police and the Director of Al-Amin in Babylon. After greeting them I was escorted by the Director to the second floor of the hospital where the main surgical theatres were located.

On the way up he explained that the patient was Colonel Taher, His Excellency the President's first cousin. The official story was that he 'accidentally' shot himself in the back whilst he was bird hunting at Al Mussayeb. He told me that my surgical colleagues had taken him straight to theatre but that the Mayor personally had requested that I be there to provide expert help.

The entrance to theatre was also packed with military uniforms; soldiers were armed with automatic guns in their hands. One of Saddam's family bodyguards made a space for me to pass and escorted me straight into theatre. The theatre, a room which was supposed to be completely sterile – in which we wore our sterile theatre blues – was now full of dirty, armed bodyguards.

Four general surgeons, six anaesthetists and all the nursing staff were packed around the operating table. It was pure chaos, pure panic. There was no organisation, no leadership, no plan and everybody was walking around asking how the injured felt.

It was a non-productive effort. Everybody seemed to pretend that they were doing something important but actually no progress had been made; it was clear that nobody wanted to take the fall if a mistake was made.

I approached the patient and introduced myself as he Head of the Surgical Division. Then I looked around at everybody that was standing watching, they looked as though they thought they were protecting him from an assassination. I suddenly found my professional personality override the political set-up and I forgot the politeness that would normally be required when addressing such men.

'What the hell is this?' I shouted. 'What do think you are all doing? This is a sterile environment to safeguard the patient and your dirty shoes and your guns are exposing him to infection. You are stealing the oxygen that he so desperately needs. Can everybody except for my five colleagues,' I pointed out two surgeons, two anaesthetists and senior theatre nurse, 'leave now please.'

I don't know how I did it. The words came out of my mouth faster than my brain could think. There was an awkward silence. Presidential guards were not used to receiving orders from anybody but their own superiors. I continued in a more assertive tone.

'If you do not leave this room now this man will certainly die.'

Everyone began to head reluctantly towards the door and out of the theatre. The injured patient suddenly piped up to add his voice.

'Everybody out now, listen to the Doctor'.

The pace immediately picked up and the room was empty within five seconds. I went to change into my theatre blues and ordered the nurses to disinfect the theatre and remove any equipment that had been touched by the gathering. My colleagues clearly thoroughly enjoyed the silence, and when we were alone they looked at me with an admiring smile and congratulated me for my words.

We now had the peace we needed to focus on the case. My colleagues began filling me in on what they already knew. A bullet had been fired into his back but there was no exit wound. They had not been able to perform a thorough examination amid the chaos so I asked the patient to tell me as much as he could.

'I was sitting next to the driver in the 4x4 and we were trying to shoot birds from the side window,' he said. 'There was an automatic gun behind my seat and as we went over a big bump I heard a loud shot at the back of the car and immediately felt something scratch my back. When I put my hand there, there was hardly any blood but I realised that something had ripped through my shirt. When I tried to get out of the car, my legs gave way and I passed out. Then I woke up here, Doctor'.

I asked if he had any specific pain now and he said that he just felt heavy and full in his stomach. I told him that in order to help him we would have to remove his shirt and trousers to investigate thoroughly. I explained that the bullet may have done some serious damage inside his body. He was very obliging and extremely polite.

A full and thorough assessment showed that he had slight weakness in his left lower limb. He had not been catheterised so his bladder was distended with urine and he had some tenderness in the lower abdomen. There was also some sensation loss in the upper part of his left leg. The bullet injury was 2-3cm to the left of the mid-line. It had most probably caused some bleeding and a clot that was pressing on the spinal cord. It did not look as if he had completely transacted his spinal cord.

I explained to him the need to put in a catheter. When the bladder drained it was full of blood. I could tell immediately that the bullet had gone through his back and into his bladder; I knew that on its passage through his body the bullet must have passed through the rectum and injured it severely.

It was a very serious situation, as the bowel continuity would have to be diverted into a bag. In other words, he would need to have a colostomy. I explained this to him and mentioned the colostomy, which I expected him to refuse.

Colostomies were almost always rejected by my Iraqi patients, even if they were life saving. In fact, people had asked me to leave them to die rather than perform a colostomy on them. Moreover, this was no ordinary patient, it as the President's cousin. I knew I would have to respect his first answer without question. I was surprised when he told me to do what I thought was best.

'I am putting my life in your hands,' he said.

It turned out that nobody had done an x-ray on him, so I asked for the mobile x-ray unit to be brought into theatre. An abdominal x-ray showed that the rectum had been perforated and damaged by the bullet. I insisted that he have the operation.

'You know, Doctor,' he said with a smile on his face, 'this is the first time in my life that somebody is giving me orders. Do the operation and don't leave the hospital until I recover and talk to you'.

I wanted to return his sense of humour.

'So, now you are giving me orders, Sir, things are clearly back to normal'.

We finished operating at midnight. We found that the bullet had entered just left of the spinal cord, into the abdomen through the rectum and was sitting in the bladder. I repaired the rectal and bladder injuries, took out the bullet and gave him a colostomy.

He was taken into Intensive Care. As soon as he woke up, he requested to see me. When I came to his bedside, he held my hand and pressed on it hard. I really felt genuine warmth as he spoke to me, with tears in his eyes.

'Thank you, Doctor,' was all that he could manage.

As I was by his side the Managing Director walked in and told me that I was needed in the Director's office on the first floor. I went down to the room, which was still heavily packed with government officials and the Mayor was holding the phone receiver towards me.

'Ismaiel,' he said, 'the Minister of Defence, Adnan Telfah, the first cousin of your patient, would like to speak to you or one of the surgeons involved'.

I took the receiver.

'Good evening, Doctor Ismaiel,' the Minister said. 'I would like to thank you and your colleagues for saving his life.'

'Sir,' I said, 'we have done our duty and I am glad to say that the operation was successful. He is fully awake in Intensive Care and does not seem to have any complications'.

'Good,' the Minister of Defence said. 'I am on my way by helicopter. I will be there in an hour. Please do not leave the hospital until I arrive.'

I put the phone down and turned to the Mayor, who had been sitting behind the Director's desk since I had arrived.

'I want to go home for a quick supper,' I said. 'I will be back soon.'

The Mayor smiled but the Managing Director answered quickly, 'Ismaiel, we have orders, nobody is to leave the hospital. It is surrounded by military personnel and we have no say in the matter. We will bring you the best food and drink and I will send somebody...' Before he could finish, the Mayor, who was Saddam's brother-in-law, interrupted.

'I don't think Doctor Ismaiel wants food or drink! I think he is missing the Madam and his daughters.'

Then he turned back to me.

'Doctor, your wife and children will be brought here in five minutes if you would like.'

I politely turned down his offer, as I didn't want to bring Mary and the kids to the hospital and expose them to the potential danger of the situation.

The phone rang again and this time it was Haythem, the eldest son of the previous President, Mr Al-Baker. Again, he asked to speak to me and with genuine gratitude and warmth he thanked me for what I had done. He told me that he was also on his way to the hospital.

The hospital car-park was cleared of vehicles and people, and properly lit, ready for a helicopter landing. After some time all the government officials in the Director's office rushed out to the car-park. I decided to go to my office instead of running to greet people that I did not know. Within minutes the Managing Director burst into my office, telling me to rush downstairs.

'Oday is here, he has turned up without warning.'

I knew that this was one man that I would have to greet. I stood up and reluctantly walked down to the main hospital entrance to 'welcome' Saddam Hussein's son.

He walked in a very relaxed fashion as though he were here for a television interview. He didn't ask about his Uncle and didn't really seem to care. He was joking around with all of the government officials that had lined up to see him. His laugh was frighteningly similar to that of his Father's; a sickly chuckle that had devilish undertones to it.

Once he had finished playing around, he was escorted towards the staircase by the most alert bodyguards. When we saw him coming towards us, both the Managing Director and I moved aside, as we had never met him before and had no reason to get in his way.

Oday had brought with him a surgical team from Baghdad, headed by Professor Raheem, one of the most senior and well known surgeons in Iraq, who also happened to be one of Saddam's private surgeons. Oday had also brought the Director of the Military Medical Directorate.

Professor Raheem was one of my surgical tutors at medical school. I had also been a sixth year medical student under his care on the surgical wards 11 and 12 at Al Jamhori Teaching Hospital. In addition, he knew my family and my father well. I thanked God that he was the medical expert that Oday had brought with him, as no doubt he was there to check out my work.

Oday greeted his uncle and gave him the usual Iraqi three kisses on his cheek before calling in Professor Raheem. He asked him to assess the patient and read the operative notes.

The room was silent until Oday spoke.

'Where is Doctor Ismaiel Bhayah'

I was on the back row of the crowd that had now gathered in the Intensive Care unit.

'Here, Sir,' I said from the back of the room, separated from Oday by the large number of bodyguards. A clearing was made and I walked towards him. He extended his hand to me.

'my uncle said you saved his life,' he said. 'Thank you Doctor. I would like you to join your colleague, Professor Raheem, whilst he assesses the patient.'

With his superb reputation, Professor Raheem, as I expected, had a look at the notes and the patient. Within a minute or so, he turned to Oday.

'If it was not for Doctor Bhayah, these injuries could have been life-threatening. I can see that he and his surgical team did a fantastic job. Ismaiel was a superb student and junior Doctor, and now as a senior surgeon he is simply brilliant.'

It was quite a testimony to hear from the leading surgeon in the country, in front of the most feared son of the President. I was in desperate need of such praise in order to calm my colleagues and myself. Oday nodded with approval and asked me when I thought they could transfer him back to Baghdad.

'He needs a couple of hours to recover before we can transfer him by air ambulance,' I said. 'If you wish, Sir, I can send a full surgical team with him in the helicopter.'

Oday shook his head.

'Doctor, Uncle Taher wants you with him on the transfer. I am sure you know how much we would all appreciate that.'

Once again I had found myself in a situation I could not get out of. I smiled.

'Of course, Sir, it would be my absolute pleasure.'

Of course, I was lying. I could think of nothing worse. It was the early hours of the morning when Oday and his entourage started to head out of the hospital to their fleet of cars. Professor Raheem lagged slightly behind Oday and whispered in my ear.

'Ismaiel, do you want anything from him? This is your moment, don't miss it.'

'Like what?'

'Anything, literally anything; a car, a house, a boat, a private jet,' he joked, 'just say it before he gets into the car'.

'Well, honestly Sir, I had planned to build my own private hospital in Hilla, which will be the first outside of Baghdad. But as you know, the Ministry of Health have stated that a minimum of four Doctors are needed to build a private hospital.'

My application had already been refused twice by the Minister of Health, but I thought it was worth dropping in conversation to Professor Raheem. Oday was up ahead shaking hands with the crowd of people, and about to get into a car when Professor Raheem ran up to him.

'Mr Oday,' he said. 'Doctor Ismaiel wants to build a private hospital in Babylon, but the Minister of Health will not allow him to'.

Before Professor Raheem finished, Oday turned to one of the bodyguards and asked him for a notebook and pen.

'Do you have land to build the hospital on?' Oday said, without looking up from the pad of paper.

'No, Sir, 'I said, 'all the suitable locations are restricted for government buildings'.

As I was talking I could tell he wasn't listening to me. He wrote on a piece of paper with a gold pen, folded it up and handed it to me without uttering a word. He got into the car and the fleet of black Mercedes sped away from the hospital. As soon as he was out of sight, I unfolded the paper to find a note written in red ink:

'Give Dr Ismaiel Bhayah any piece of land he wants and allow him to build his own private hospital'.

That was it. One sentence with a barely legible signature underneath. No headed paper, no official government stamp, not even a date. I could have written the thing myself.

I didn't sleep that night. Mary and I kept staring at the piece of paper with Oday's scribbles on. We had no idea that we were in possession of a ticket to our dream hospital.

The following day, I went to the Director of the Municipality in Babylon. He not only knew my family well, but had already seen my face from frequent visits asking about buying land to build a hospital on. I didn't need to explain why I was back to ask again. The rumour about my note had spread like wildfire. The whole of Babylon was talking about my meeting with Oday.

We had a cup of tea in his office and then he took me in the car with one of the Land Registry experts. We drove around Hilla and he pointed out all of the available sites. I now had the choice of every single strategic government plot available. I eventually chose a 4,000m^2 site free of charge in the most strategic location in Babylon.

A week later, I got permission from the Minister of Health to build a hospital in my own name. I was the only Doctor in

Iraq who was granted permission at that time to build a hospital alone, and not as a group of four. The scrap piece of paper that Oday had given me was the key that I needed to unlock every government door. Thereafter, I was treated like royalty at every government office and given the paperwork and permission I needed without delay.

When I began building the hospital, essential materials like bricks, cement and steel rods were very scarce. Most people had to wait up to twelve months to get five thousand bricks delivered. I needed much more than that for my hospital. I had planned to build twenty-five single rooms, two theatre suites, one Intensive Care unit, one delivery suite, two four-bedded bays, one out-patient department, one kitchen, one laundry room and one store room to the back.

I was given all the building materials I required within one month of ordering them. I had ample supplies of bricks, steel and cement. I even built two big apartments above the hospital. One was for the foreign Doctors and nurses working in the hospital and the other was a three-bedroom luxury flat for Mary and my daughters. I wanted somewhere for them to stay so that when I was working long hours I could go upstairs to spend some time with all my lovely girls and they would not be alone in our big house.

The hospital was designed by Mary and myself; we wanted it to be a very Arabic building made up of arches and large round pillars.

At the same time that I was building my hospital, Saddam was also building one of his palaces in Babylon. The local government brick factory director in Mahaweel told me that there were special bricks made for the President's palace on which the words 'built in Saddam Hussein's era' were inscribed on the face. He showed me one of the bricks and they were beautiful. He offered to inscribe my name on the bricks for my hospital so that they would be there for all future generations to see. I knew it was risky accepting his offer as Saddam would not accept anybody trying to copy his elite, prestigious and unique style of life. However I had fallen in love with the design of the bricks and wanted my hospital to carry my name.

And I was right. The day after the bricks were delivered to the site, the Director of Al-Amin, a good friend of mine, contacted me to say that the director of the brick factory had made a grave mistake by making bricks with my name on and had been arrested. He informed me that they were sending a bulldozer to crush the five thousand bricks that had been left on my land.

I took Mary and my brother Ahmed to the building site and we managed to get about two hundred bricks into the back of our cars before the bulldozer arrived to crush them.

Saddam was unaware that I actually used those bricks to put in the foundation layer of the hospital. We also put a time capsule under the foundations with pictures and a newspaper cutting from that day. Both still lie in the ruins of the hospital in Babylon.

THE BAD

The Minister of Health

Dr Ibrahim, the Minister of Health from 1978, was a very highly respected and educated gynaecologist who was continuously praised by Health Department employees across the country and loved by everyone that met him.

He was the descendent of a famous family tribe in the west of Iraq. He was modest, down-to-earth, considerate and very well-spoken. He was a huge credit to Iraq as the Minister of Health and had given the Health Service its golden era. He was chosen for the post by the previous President, President Al-Baker, who had put a great deal of pressure on him to accept the position in the first place.

To improve the health service, Dr Ibrahim cut down the useless bureaucracy and gave hospitals great independence. He was the first Minister of Health to encourage creative thought and acknowledge the achievements of Doctors and nurses. In spite of his ministerial duties he did not give up clinical practice, dedicating his life completely to the Iraqi people. Dr Ibrahim was always available to help those in need whether they were patients or employees. Although he was from such a well-known and wealthy family he never abused his position or prioritised money over good deeds.

In 1982, Iraqi radio and television stations announced the execution of the Minister of Health due to negligence. They alleged that some vials had been imported into Iraq which contained a very high dose of intra-venous potassium chloride, leading to the deaths of hundreds of patients, in civilian and military hospitals. Dr Ibrahim had supposedly been warned about these vials, but ignored the warning and the vials had been distributed to hospitals.

I knew straight away that the story did not add up. I was Clinical Director of Surgery in my hospital at the time and don't ever recall my hospital being given different potassium chloride vials to those that we had always had.

Besides that, I knew full well that the Minister of Health had nothing to do with the dosage of the drugs that were imported. He would simply authorise the orders. It had always been the responsibility of the Department of Drug Control to ensure that the dosage of drugs was correct. Something like this would not have escaped their attention. Not only that, but Dr Ibrahim was known for being very critical of taking orders that he felt were not in scope of his job. He would never have taken on such a responsibility.

Everybody quietly knew that the negligence story was a cover up for something much more serious and twisted. Except for those unfortunate enough to witness it, nobody else in Iraq or the outside world was able to find out the real cause of the minister's execution.

A very close friend of mine fell into that category and entrusted me with the story. He was later killed in very suspicious circumstances. I had no reason to doubt my friend's account of the events and to this day I have never heard anything to make me believe that it happened otherwise.

He was in the room that day and here is his account of the incident. In 1981, President Khomeini, the Islamic Leader of Iran, a personal enemy of Saddam Hussein, had declared that he was prepared to stop the fighting providing that Saddam stepped aside and allowed somebody else to be the leader of Iraq. Saddam called an urgent meeting with the Revolutionary Leadership Assembly, all of whom were very highly ranked Ba'ath Party members.

Together they constituted what was known as the Revolutionary Leadership Assembly. Dr Ibrahim was present at that meeting. As usual, they sat at a large round table and Saddam began chairing the meeting.

'Well Comrades,' he said. 'I have heard what Khomeini demands. He will stop the war if I step down as leader and let somebody else take my place. I have called this meeting to understand your thoughts on this and get your suggestions on what we should do.'

He said that Saddam seemed very relaxed and calm; he sat back in his chair waiting to hear from the group. The Ba'ath Party members knew all too well that they were not supposed to have their own opinions and kept their mouths shut. Dr Ibrahim, as an intelligent man, was confident with putting forward an idea.

'Well, Sir, the Iranians and their leader Khomeini are stubborn, strict, religious Shia's. This war has already claimed a huge loss of life on both sides. Perhaps we could pretend that you have stepped down to stop the war, and when things settle you could officially resume your position as our leader.'

'And who, Doctor, do you suggest should temporarily replace me?' Saddam asked calmly.

Dr Ibrahim put forward a name from the Common Council who was a Shia from the south. He thought that such a person might be more readily accepted by the Iranian regime. Saddam addressed the table.

'Okay, Comrades,' he said. 'We have a good idea here. Who else thinks that I should step down temporarily?'

Promptly all the members of the Ba'ath Party expressed total rejection to the idea. The Vice President answered, 'We will not support this, Sir. You are the only Leader and we will fight for you until every drop of blood has been shed. We will not allow you to step down, even if you want to. This country and its people need you, Sir'.

The answer was so rehearsed and so emotionless, but it was the answer that Saddam wanted to hear. The President stood up and walked into an adjacent room. His Head of Security came out to where the men were sitting and called Dr Ibrahim through to the same room.

The Council members sat in silence until a gunshot echoed against the walls. Saddam casually walked back into the room, returning his pistol into its holster, making sure that everybody saw him do so. He sat back down, leant back, lit a cigar and continued.

'Any other ideas?' he said.

As the meeting went on, Dr Ibrahim's body was dragged out of the room from behind where Saddam sat. He had been shot in the head.

His name went down in the history of Saddam's era as a traitor and nobody spoke of his good deeds again. Every Iraqi knew deep in their hearts that his execution was not only a sad loss to his family but to the country as a whole. He was one of the best Ministers of Health in the recent history of Iraq. He was a man of principle and, in my eyes, a hero to be able to stand tall against Saddam; I would hope that history will remember him in this way.

Doctor Aziz

When I was a medical student in Baghdad, Dr Aziz was one of the best teachers at the school. He had a very gentle character, was nicely spoken and always dressed smartly. He was modest and had very high medical standards and ethics; he also mixed well with both junior and senior staff. He too had done his training and gained his qualifications from the UK and was quite simply the best in his field.

After I qualified from medical school and came to England to study in 1970, I met Dr Aziz twice in London, both times accompanied by a mutual friend whom we both knew very well. Dr Aziz was very sociable and had a great sense of humour.

In 1979, he was chosen to be one of the President's private specialists. To be a private Doctor for the President was a very enviable position because it gave you automatic privileges wherever you went. However, it also carried its burdens.

Being so close to the President meant that you were very closely watched. You also had to be available at all hours of the day to attend to the President and his family, and therefore give up your own life for him. Through his position Dr Aziz's wife became a very close friend to the First Lady and they frequently went on holiday together, shopping in London and Paris.

When my eldest daughter, May, was six years-old, she developed a verruca on the sole of her foot, which made it painful to walk and stopped her from going to school. Initial treatment in Babylon by a few of my colleagues did not give a successful result and it became a real problem.

Eventually I decided to take her to see Dr Aziz, who I knew was practicing at the Central Clinic for Skin Diseases in the *Al-Saadoon* area of Baghdad. He was both the Director and a practitioner for the centre. I was given a warm welcome from him.

In spite of his busy clinic, he was typically Arabic with his hospitality, even if it meant delaying his appointments. We chatted about the good old days and how we should meet up more often. He then took a look at the verruca on May's foot and told me that he would need to remove it under a general anaesthetic as it was now deep into her foot.

He prescribed her some local application to soften it up. He also told me that he was going to London for three weeks, but when he was back in September, if the local application didn't improve the verruca, he would remove it before she went back to school. I thanked him and we exchanged telephone numbers, arranging to meet up at my orchard on the Euphrates in Babylon.

May started to use the ointment he gave her and the verruca got better, but it did not disappear entirely and was painful for her. So, at the beginning of September I rang the centre to arrange an appointment. I was told that there were no available appointments.

Every time I rang they said that he was not there and that I should not call back. After a few attempts of trying to get hold of him, I decided to ring his home number. A lady answered the phone. When I introduced myself and asked to speak to Dr Aziz, she started to cry.

'I am sorry Doctor, he is not here. Please don't call again.'

She hung up in a panic and I knew immediately that something was wrong. I decided that I would head to Baghdad for myself and go to his house to see if he was okay. I packed some presents and boxes of fresh fruit from my orchard. Before setting off, I rang our mutual friend, who was also a relative of Dr Aziz, to see if he wanted to join me.

When I rang him he was very vague and kept changing the subject. I realised that he didn't want to talk on the phone because the lines must have been tapped, so I apologised for all the questions and said goodbye. After I put the phone down I drove to his house in Baghdad and he led me into the sitting room where we stayed for the entirety of my visit.

He was frightened to talk in the garden in case anybody overheard.

'You need to stop asking questions,' he told me. 'Dr Aziz was executed by Saddam. Have you not heard the story?'

I felt sick as the words came out of his mouth. I knew something was not right but this was the last thing that I had expected. He was not only his private dermatologist but also a close family friend. What could he have possibly done wrong to deserve death? My friend asked me to promise that I would never repeat the story, and explained that he was putting his own life in jeopardy by telling me. He wanted me to stop asking around for Dr Aziz before I became a target myself.

To explain what had happened, he told me that while he was in London Dr Aziz had been to a private party at a friend's house. After a few drinks, when everybody was relaxed, they had started to talk about life in Iraq. At the party, people started asking Dr Aziz what it was like to work for the President.

In a sarcastic tone, one person asked what Saddam could possibly need him for, when there were hardly any life threatening skin problems to be called out for. Doctor Aziz, with his usual wit and humour replied; 'I get called in to treat their venereal diseases'. People laughed and continued the night by eating, drinking and having fun.

When his holiday ended, Dr Aziz flew back to Iraq, arriving at Saddam International Airport. As he stepped off the aeroplane, he could see his family waiting for him. But before he could reach them he was arrested by two soldiers and taken away. His family were told that he had been taken to the Al-Amin to answer a few queries and would be sent home later that day.

Two weeks passed and Dr Aziz never contacted his family. Not knowing where her husband was, his wife got desperate and called Saddam's wife to ask for help. The First Lady couldn't give her any answers and suggested that she came to see Saddam for herself.

When Saddam sat with her he immediately said, 'Do you accept that your husband has been talking about us abroad? That he has been saying we have venereal diseases in public? Is that the treatment I expect from such a close professional and family friend?' His wife began to deny that he would say such a thing and told Saddam how much respect and praise for him her husband harboured. How he loved Saddam's family as if they were his own. She said that maybe people that were jealous of his position had tried to get him into trouble.

Saddam brought out a tape player onto the desk. The room was silent, and then she heard the voice of her husband at the party – weeks previously and thousands of miles away in London making the joke about Saddam. She nearly collapsed. She begged Saddam for forgiveness, telling him to fire her husband immediately and to strike him off from medical practice. She pleaded with him to bring her husband home because her children missed their father greatly.

'I appeal to your kindness to forgive him Your Excellency. He must have learnt a lesson by now and I promise you he will repay you for his mistake.'

Saddam thought for a moment and said 'Go home now, and I will send him to you tomorrow'. She thanked the President for his kindness and understanding and rushed home to tell the children the good news.

Just as Saddam promised, her husband was sent home the following day. When she heard the military car pull up outside, she gathered her children and ran to the front door. Dr Aziz's body lay in a box on the door step with a bullet to the head.

Persian Origins

After our son Marwan's death in 1979, we decided to leave my father's big house to temporarily rent somewhere until we had built our own house. We wanted to get away from all the memories of Marwan and everything that reminded us of him at my father's house. I used to spend endless, sleepless nights walking around hearing his voice and his laugher echoing off the walls.

I moved with Mary and my daughter May to a rented house in a nice province of Hilla called Haybabel. It was an exclusive area in Babylon, right on the bank of the Euphrates, where most of the upper-class and famous people lived. Our neighbours were really nice and welcoming. Some of them cooked dinner for us on our first day, other brought us presents and some invited us to their own houses to meet with their families.

Our immediate next door neighbour was a young housewife called Fatima. She was nearly the same age as Mary and they became very good friends. During the day when her husband I and were at work, Mary and Fatima used to chat across the low fence in the garden or visit each other, gossiping over tea and sweets. Fatima had two young boys; one was four years-old and the other was one year-old, and we had May who at the time who was only a few months old. Fatima's husband was a secondary school teacher of history and religion. He was very quiet, highly educated and could talk about anything, but he didn't have much of a sense of humour.

A few months after we had moved in, I came back from work to eat lunch with Mary and found Fatima and her two children sitting in the kitchen. She was in a desperate state. As soon as I walked in, I asked what was wrong.

'Please, Doctor,' she pleaded, 'my husband was taken from school as he was leaving his morning class. His colleagues saw him get pushed into a white VW Passat; an Al-Amin car. I went to their offices and then to the police and the Mayor, and they denied all knowledge of the incident. I know you have contacts and I would kiss your hands if you could find my husband'.

Then, she began to cry hysterically.

After I asked her a few questions to verify the story, I went straight to the phone and rang my friend, the Chief of Al-Amin.

'Honestly, Dr Ismaiel, I don't know what you are talking about. I wouldn't lie about taking him, we don't fear anyone. It sounds like her husband has personal problems and people may have kidnapped him for a different reason. Please warn her that she needs to stop blaming the government'.

I knew immediately that he was lying, but I also knew that the call was being monitored so I put the phone down. When I rang the police department and the Mayor's office I got exactly the same answers: her husband had vanished without a trace.

I tried my best to comfort her. I said I would continue my efforts to find out where her husband was and offered her my full support for anything she may need. We started to think about whether he had any enemies that could have done this, but really we all knew that this sort of kidnapping was not allowed under Saddam. It had to be a government job.

In that year President Saddam Hussein had started deporting all Shea's from the south, whose nationality certificate did not state that they were descendants of the Ottoman Empire. The government claimed that the Shea's of Persian origin were only loyal to Iran and to the militant rulers of Iran, so all the men below the age of fifty and male children in their teens had to be deported.

Wives, daughters and very young boys had to stay behind in Iraq. Thousands of people from Babylon had been deported to Iran in that manner, and the effect on the women and children who were left behind was devastating.

Seven specialists from my hospital were taken in one day. We never saw them again and neither did their families. I was sure that the rest of the world, especially the Arabic and Islamic world, were fully aware of this extreme, inhumane and brutal behaviour, but they never dared to condemn it or even mention it in the media. The world stood by and let Saddam torture the Iraqis in every way possible, and this was just one more regulation that we were supposed to suffer in silence.

I had a feeling that Fatima's husband had been taken under this regulation.

Over the following months, Fatima had no choice but to come to terms with the fact that her husband was gone. My efforts to find out what had happened to him were futile and Fatima realised that, despite the psychological trauma she was experiencing, she had to live on for her children.

She registered them at school and nursery. A year later, in order to support her family, she started working as a clerk at the bank. When we moved to our new house in 1981, we promised Fatima that we would keep in touch and help her whenever we could.

Two years later, her eldest son had turned six and the youngest boy was three. She received a letter from Al-Amin asking her to bring her children to their offices in Babylon to visit their father. The first people she broke the good news to were Mary and I. Fatima was ecstatic. We were so happy for her because she could finally resume her life as normal. Most importantly, the boys would get their father back.

Fatima got the children ready in their best clothes and explained that they were going to see their father. They had made him a card and she had stuck pictures of her husband on their t-shirts so that he would see how much they had all missed him. Fatima herself bought a new outfit, handbag and did her hair to look as best she could to see her husband again.

On the day, they walked to Al-Amin, which was only one kilometre away from her house. At the reception she introduced herself and showed the letter she had received to bring her children to meet their father. The man at the desk instructed her that the boys were to go in first.

As a woman she was to see her husband separately in a private room after their reunion. She agreed to let the boys go in first, not wanting to mess up her chance to see her husband again. She explained to the boys that they were going into a room to see their dad, then she kissed them on the head before handing them over to a security guard.

Fatima sat and waited in the reception area. After two hours, when there was no sign of the boys, she really began to panic. She asked the receptionist how long he thought they would be. The man behind the desk told her not to worry and that it was probably an emotional reunion for her husband.

An hour after this, the receptionist finished his shift and started packing to go home. He handed over to a new officer, who settled behind the desk. Only a few minutes later he looked up at Fatima.

'What are you doing here, lady?'

'Waiting for my children, Sir,' she answered. 'They have gone into that room to see their father.'

He looked down at the paperwork in front of him.

'What children?' he replied.

Fatima walked towards the desk and showed him the letter she had received, and a photo of her husband. He took them from her, ripped them up and dropped them on the floor.

'This is a government office lady, not a nursery. Get out! Now!'

Panic took over and Fatima started pleading with the man.

'Okay sir, please just give me my children back. I don't need to see my husband.'

She went to kiss his hand in a desperate appeal for mercy, but he pulled his hand away and did not acknowledge her plea.

'If my husband is a traitor then imprison him, but please, leave my boys, they are all I have.'

Without warning the security guard came to escort her out of the building and dragged her onto the street.

It was then that she came to my house, not knowing who else to turn to. I had just woken up from my afternoon siesta and was getting ready to go to work when she pulled up in a taxi and hysterically told me the whole story. I got on the phone straight away to the Al-Amin offices. Taking her husband was one thing, but to take her young boys in such a cruel manner was unforgivable.

With anger, I explained the story to the new Head of Security at Al-Amin and asked him to help a grieving and, desperate mother. I appealed to him as a parent and as a father, but it was useless.

These men had been trained to have no emotion whatsoever. There was no human side to appeal to. He told me that her husband had asked to take the boys back to Iran.

'We can't do anything, Doctor, it was the father's choice. He felt the boys would be better off with him. It was a very emotional reunion and he insisted on taking them immediately. Please tell the lady to relax and that her boys are safe.'

I ended the call, completely unconvinced with the story, but told Fatima exactly what he had told me. She began wailing and screaming on my kitchen floor. There was absolutely nothing we could do or say to console her. I had never felt so utterly helpless; I wasn't sure how much more suffering one person could take.

I left it a few hours before trying to call some more of my contacts. If we could not get the boys back, at least I could give her peace of mind by finding out what really happened.

Fatima had been to the Mayor, written to Saddam and called at every government office but got nowhere. Everybody denied knowledge of both her husband and her young children. Mary stayed at her house to try and comfort her, but it was the most heart-breaking thing to watch. She had nothing and no one.

Years passed and Fatima consoled herself by knowing that all her boys were now together and safe in Iran. Mary and I supported her closely and made sure that she knew we would look after her.

We did our best to convince her that the boys were probably better off living in Iran than under Saddam, even though we did not believe that ourselves. From that time on Fatima always dressed in black, mourning the loss of her husband and children.

It was in 1987 when Fatima received a letter from the Security Directorate in Babylon, which enclosed the death certificate for her husband dated 1981. Inside the envelope was the bullet used to shoot him, and a bill for the cost of the bullet.

Saddam would send these to the families of those that he executed to insult them; to show that their loved ones were not even worth the price of the 50p bullet put into their head.

Fatima reached an uncontrollable state of emotion and again came straight to my house. Mary and I were lost for words, if her husband had been shot dead in 1981, then who had she taken her children to meet in 1983? She was already a broken woman and this pushed her to the absolute edge. I couldn't understand why Saddam wanted to play with a poor, weak and helpless woman in that way. If her husband had been against the government, why involve his four and six year-old boys?

Every part of me wished that she had never opened that letter, that she could go on believing that her boys were in Iran with their father. But now she knew the twisted truth and could not settle until she found her boys.

I cannot explain in words how Fatima looked when she sat in front of us, absorbing the truth. I sat her down, looked into her eyes and told her exactly what I would do in her situation.

'Fatima, you have nothing left to lose. This ruthless regime has taken everything from you. It is not Al-Amin making the decisions, it is the Big Man. Go to his palace and do whatever it takes to speak to him. Find the answers and find the children.'

When I finished talking, she appeared strangely calm. Without any emotion on her face, she spoke as if hypnotised.

'Doctor, I will go to Baghdad. I will do whatever it costs. I need to know that if anything happens to me you will tell my story. I want people to know the truth about my husband.'

Fatima went straight to the Republican Palace in Baghdad and asked to see Saddam. The guard at the gate slapped her across the face for using his name without his title.

'Be polite, you bitch, when you refer to Saddam. Refer to him as his title, His Excellency. Has he asked to see you? Where is your letter?'

'I don't need a letter,' she said. 'He killed my husband and took my children. I demand to see him now.'

She continued to refer to him by his first name to provoke a response. The soldiers laughed in her face and she threw herself on the floor and laid across the entrance to the palace.

She knew they would not take her seriously so started to threaten to take her clothes off, knowing full well the shame and dishonour it would bring to the Arab men around her and in particular to Saddam's palace. The soldiers knew they would be in trouble if Saddam found that a woman was taking her clothes off outside his palace and making a mockery of him in public.

However, every time they went to remove her she threatened to remove her clothing. The soldiers began to panic and tried to negotiate with her, promising her that she could speak to one of the President's advisors at some point that week. Fatima was not prepared to see anybody but Saddam and she was certainly not prepared to wait.

After she was there for a few hours, a black Mercedes appeared from under the palace grounds and headed towards her. The front door was flung open and the driver shouted at her to get in. She clambered into the car and sat next to the driver.

It was Saddam.

She tried to kiss his hands out of respect and desperation, but he pushed her away.

'Calm down and tell me what I can do for you,' he said.

As he started driving away from the palace with just the two of them in the car, Fatima explained the situation to him.

'Sir, when God takes the lives of our loved ones he always gives us the strength and ability to cope with the loss, but when you or any other human takes their life you don't have the ability to do that.'

Saddam smiled at her. 'Go home,' he said. 'I will contact you within the next twenty-four hours personally. Let me make some enquiries about your children.'

'Sorry Sir, I am staying here. I am your shadow. I am not going anywhere. Sir, I know you can find my children and I am prepared to hold their dead bodies, but I just want to hug them, I want to mourn them, I want to bury them, I want to know what happened to them. I am a mother and I can't go on not knowing, it is killing me inside.'

'Okay,' he said, 'don't go back to Babylon. I will get my men to take you to one of our guest hotels and I promise I will contact you as soon as I have found your boys.'

Fatima said that she really believed him from the sincerity in his voice and knew that she could not ask for more than words at that point.

He drove them back to the palace and another car took her to a local hotel. She stayed awake through the night, waiting for a phone call to tell her about the fate of her children.

At 5 a.m. two men in military uniforms came to the hotel, picked her up and drove her to the Iranian border. At 7 a.m. they arrived at Mandalay, and she could see a Land Rover waiting. The cars signalled to each other, flashing their lights, and two boys got out of the Land Rover.

She watched as the boys were pushed forwards, towards her car. They walked slowly and kept looking back at the man who had driven them there. When they were close enough she could see that they were her children. Tall, pale and extremely underweight, they were almost unrecognisable. She ran towards them. She told me that it was a feeling that she would never be able to put into words, to have her children back in her arms again. She told me that she didn't cry, she just took them to her chest, to her heart.

I remember her telling me that she wanted to squeeze them so tight that they disappeared inside her heart and nobody could ever take them away from her again. It was the only way she could describe her feelings at that time.

She told me how the boys didn't react at all. They kept quiet and emotionless, never uttering a word. They didn't raise their arms to hug her and didn't shed a tear. For Fatima it was like holding two lifeless, dead bodies.

It had emerged that the boys did not understand what their mother was saying because they had forgotten their Arabic and only spoke Persian. Her boys had been left in Iran from the ages of three and six to fend for themselves, to beg on the streets and to struggle to survive through each day.

When Fatima realised what they had been through, she collapsed with spasmodic crying. They drove out of Mandalay town, back to Hilla. On the way she bought them kebab sandwiches, cans of coke, a banana and an orange each. They had never had a full can of coke or a whole fruit to themselves since they were thrown across the border.

When she got back home the emptiness of her life without her husband dawned on her. Although she was happy to have her children back, she realised that her life would never again be complete.

'When they arrived home,' she told me, 'the eldest boy walked straight into the house. He knew his way. He was looking around, looking at the old photos and then he walked upstairs straight to the bedroom that I had shared with his father. He was expressionless, as though sleepwalking. He came downstairs and took me by the hand, wanting me to follow him.'

She told me how she grabbed the younger boy and they both followed him to a picture upstairs. The photo was of all the family. He placed his finger on his dad. 'He asked something in Persian and I guessed he was wondering where that man was.

The picture had been taken one year before his father was killed, one year before our lives were utterly destroyed. I couldn't tolerate it and I broke down, letting out the past eight years of sorrow. I buried my face in the pillow, sobbing. I felt the eldest boy's little hand stroke my hair and I cried more. Both came close to me for the first time and I laid them on my lap. I felt their hearts beating rapidly. I could easily relate to the sound of their beating hearts. It was exactly the same feeling I had had when I was pregnant with them.'

We gave Fatima money to help support her restored family; I felt it was my duty to help. In fact, I felt it was an honour. Fatima was the strongest woman I had ever met in Iraq. She had suffered at the cruel hands of Saddam for doing nothing more than marrying a man of Persian origin. But she had survived.

Only a few months after she had got them safely home, I bumped into Fatima and her sons in a supermarket. I asked her how she was coping. Fatima had focussed on rehabilitating the boys and trying to accustom them to their new Iraqi lifestyle. The main struggle for her was not being able to communicate with them.

The boys had only spoken Persian for many years, and it had taken months for her to teach them the basics of their mother tongue. It was clearly enough for them to get by, as they had greeted me competently in Arabic. It transpired that neither of the boys ever spoke of what happened to them while they were in Iran, and Fatima hoped that they had suppressed those memories.

Her strength and normality was overwhelming to me. To a passer-by she must have looked like any other mother, shopping with her sons and worrying about what to cook the family for dinner. Nobody was aware of the mental torture she had bottled up inside of her. I asked if she needed help with taking care of the children, but she graciously thanked me and declined.

Four months later, on a Friday afternoon, Fatima turned up unexpectedly at our house. She said she wanted the boys to meet the family and know how much we meant to her. We sat down and had a drink before Fatima asked her sons to go outside and play in the garden.

Fatima began to explain that she had still not been able to register the boys at school. With her husband having been branded as a traitor, she required permission from Al-Amin to allow them to enrol at school. I wasn't sure where the conversation was headed or what she expected me to do to help, but continued to listen.

The Hanging Gardens of Babylon

She told me how she had been to Al Amin almost every day to beg for a nationality certificate for the boys with no luck. Eventually she met with an officer at Al Amin and he had come to 'an agreement' with her, in return for granting the boys full Iraqi nationality and entry to one of the best schools in Babylon.

It dawned on me why she had come to my house. I had heard of men, women and children being blackmailed by the government to become undercover spies. I knew the position it forced people into, having to feed back gossip they heard from family, friends and neighbours regardless of their devotion to them.

There were stories of civilian spies being killed for not reporting back news to Al Amin what was later discovered through other sources. Fatima was not here on a social visit, but to warn me and my family of the new obligations she had had enforced on her. I made it clear to her in an indirect way, that I understood what she was trying to say and thanked her for her visit.

We didn't see Fatima often after that day. I don't know if she purposefully avoided us to reduce the risk of hearing something she would have to report back, or whether her new role had simply consumed her life.

In 1990, before I left Iraq, I went to the bank to withdraw a large sum of money. The cashier told me that the Director of the branch would have to authorise the transaction. She led me to a side door and there, in a beautiful open plan office, I found myself face to face with Fatima.

She was not the same woman that I had known. She had regained the colour in her skin and life in her eyes. She was dressed head to toe in designer labels and had a tone of authority in her voice.

'Ismaiel,' she said, 'it is so good to see you my dear friend.'

I sat down in her large office and we caught up on lost time. She filled me in on her boys' progress at school.

'My eldest has become quite an artist,' she explained, 'but he only paints dark and depressing pieces of art. It seems to be the only way he can express his suppressed emotions about what happened to them. 'As for me, 'I have done well. They have promoted me quickly and I have been given everything I could ever wish for.'

The cashier came in to hand me my money and I got up to leave Fatima in peace. As I went to say bye, she leaned in close to me.

'Don't worry, Doctor,' she whispered. 'I have not hurt anybody along the way. I'm playing their game. I lie to them as they lied to me. I'm doing it for my husband and children.'

As I left her office and headed home, her words plagued my thoughts. I wasn't sure what game she was playing with the government, or how long she would get away with doing so, but it was not my place to stop her.

THE UGLY

Solitary Confinement

My brother Ahmed served in the army for twenty-eight years and at the end of the Iran/Iraq war was released as a Colonel. He had never been a member of the Ba'ath Party and had always kept to himself. He avoided big parties and mixing with people he wasn't close to.

He was very honest, devoted and loyal to his family and his friends. He married Huda in 1975 and they had six children together: four girls and two boys. The eldest one was born in 1976 and the youngest in 1990.

Soon after their last baby was born, when his wife was only thirty-eight, she developed breast cancer and in spite of the immediate removal of her breast the disease spread. My brother called me in England, seeking help.

At the time I was working at New Cross Hospital in Wolverhampton and I advised him that unfortunately her case sounded terminal. But my brother insisted that she wanted to have all the medical treatment possible, even if it only meant extending her life by a few months. She wanted to spend as long as possible with my brother and their six children.

I arranged for her to come to England for private treatment, telling my brother that I would cover all the costs, and I sent them all that they needed to get a treatment visa to England. On their side my brother had applied for leave, even though a retired Colonel, he still required permission from the Ministry of Defence to leave Iraq.

By the time they came to leave, the cancer was so advanced that she had developed a collection of fluid in her abdomen (ascites) that needed regular tapping to relieve her pain. My brother learned to tap the ascites to drain the fluid out of her stomach whenever she felt uncomfortable.

It had to be done at home because the sanctions on Iraq had meant a shortage of everything, in particular essential medical equipment. The disposable syringes and needles that they used were given out on prescription with the provision that they were to be used twenty times before being thrown away.

The dangers associated with using the syringes in this way were life-threatening, but the government didn't care. It was just another suffering that my family and other Iraqis had to bear under the sanctions. The outside world thought that sanctions meant we stopped receiving luxury items into Iraq. Nobody talked of the real pain and suffering it inflicted, taking away the most basic amenities and medical supplies.

Of course, Saddam, his family and associates weren't ever affected by the sanctions. For them it was just a word in a dictionary. My brother would be given one syringe and one needle every fifteen days to make sure that he did not throw it away after one use.

When they were packing their bags for England, they put the one syringe and one needle that they had been given into their hand luggage and set off on their journey. As there were no flights out of Iraq, they left by coach to Jordan. This twelve hour journey was hard enough for any person to tolerate, let alone a woman suffering from the final stages of cancer.

After a ten hour drive from Baghdad they reached the Iraqi border checkpoint of Trabeel. Passengers had to check in individually inside the control building, but because Huda was too weak to even stand Ahmed left her on the bus and went to queue at the passport inspection point to receive their exit stamp. When it was his turn to approach the desk the soldier looked at my brother's passport and then up at him, and then back down to the passport before asking him what he did for a living.

'I am a retired Colonel,' Ahmed answered, and to avoid any trouble added, 'you can see that my passport has been stamped and authorised by the Ministry of Defence.

'Okay, Sir,' the soldier said, 'let me check something with my Director.'

About ten minutes later, a captain came out and invited Ahmed to go inside the office.

'Well, Sir,' the Captain said, 'your name is Ahmed Mohammed Ali. Correct?'

'Yes and no,' Ahmed replied. 'Yes, I am Ahmed Mohammed Ali, and no, because my surname is Bhayah and it is clearly listed as that on my passport.

'Correct, Sir,' the officer answered. 'I can see that your last name is Bhayah, but I have very clear orders from Al-Amin to arrest and send back to Baghdad any Iraqi under the name of Ahmed Mohammed Ali.'

It dawned on Ahmed that he was in serious trouble.

'Presumably the person you are looking for does not have the same surname, date of birth and profession as I do. Don't you think that further identification criteria should be looked at before you arrest everybody?'

Ahmed desperately hoped that the officer was listening.

'My wife is on the coach and she has terminal cancer. I am only taking her to the UK for treatment and coming straight back.'

The officer did not acknowledge Ahmed.

'I have six children, all of them below the age of fourteen,' he continued. 'I need to be with her to look after her for my children's sake. Please listen to me. My wife will die if we return to Baghdad and she will suffer in severe pain if she continues alone.'

'Believe me, Sir,' the officer replied, emotionless. 'I am very sympathetic and understanding and I wish things were in my hands to help you, but the orders I have are very clear. I am sorry to say that you are under arrest and we will be taking you back to Baghdad.'

Desperate to appeal to the officer's better nature, Ahmed began to beg.

'I have already explained, my wife can't cope without me. She is terminally ill. Please come to the coach with me and just look at her. I have to aspirate the fluid from her abdomen once or twice a day for her to even cope. She has never been abroad by herself before, even if she was fit and healthy she would be scared. Please, for the sake of humanity, give me your phone and let me speak to the Minister of Defence and he can tell you my situation. My passport was only stamped three days ago; surely they must have checked my details then?'

His efforts were futile. The men had been ordered to arrest anybody under the name Ahmed Mohammed Ali, and that was exactly what they were going to do, regardless of any further indication that my brother was not the man the government were looking for.

They didn't let Ahmed go back to the bus. Instead, they took him immediately to a car, where they blindfolded him and handcuffed his hands behind his back.

Ahmed asked them to promise that they would tell Huda that he had been delayed for questioning and that he would join her as soon as possible. He gave them her passport and all the money that he had, and asked them to promise that she would receive both.

'Tell her God will be with her and not to be frightened,' Ahmed said. 'As soon as she arrives in Jordan, please tell her to contact my brother in England immediately before going to the British Embassy.'

The soldiers did as he asked and Ahmed was driven away from the checkpoint under arrest.

The journey in the car from Trabeel to Baghdad was extremely uncomfortable for Ahmed, handcuffed and blindfolded in the back. He appealed to them to change the cuffs to the front as it was very painful but they said that they could not.

About eight hours into the journey, the car stopped and he was helped out. He was led into a building and could hear a lot of people around him. They walked him through what he suspected to be long, narrow, cold corridors. He said the place was stuffy and that every footstep gave a very loud echo in the enclosed space. He heard a very heavy metal door open and, he was pushed inside a space. His hands were un-cuffed and he was told to wait for five minutes before removing the blindfold. The heavy door was closed and locked behind him.

When he removed the blindfold a few minutes later, he was unable to see a thing. It was pitch black. He thought that it might be because his eyes had been blindfolded and that his vision would return slowly, but after a few minutes of rubbing his eyes, he remained in complete darkness.

He started to feel around him and found a small switch on the wall, which turned on a very small red light as faint as a candle. It provided enough light for him to see that he was an isolation cell in solitary confinement.

The cell was no bigger than four by six feet. No taps, no sink, no toilet; just a metal bucket in the corner. The metal door had what looked like a cat flap at the bottom. Ahmed began to feel real despair so he started knocking on the door with his hands and shouted for as long as he could.

'Help me, please help me. I am innocent. I haven't done anything and this is a big mistake. I beg you to let me out. I beg you to hold any trial or inquest, just don't leave me here. I am a Colonel in the army and I must see somebody to explain that there has been a very big mistake.'

There was no response whatsoever. Claustrophobic, frightened and worried sick for his wife, he sat on the floor and recited paragraphs from the holy book of the Koran, hoping to gain some strength and tolerance. Eventually he became so exhausted; he passed out on the cold concrete floor.

He remembers being woken by the sound of footsteps outside and a metal bowl being pushed through the flap followed by a piece of bread. He ate it all immediately. It was a bowl of very watery soup, hardly enough for a small kitten, and a quarter of Iraqi bread. His hunger pangs weren't satisfied, but he thought that it couldn't be long before they would give him lunch and supper so he could satisfy his hunger then.

He waited and waited, but nothing came and nobody contacted him. He started knocking on the metal door and this time appealed to be let out for his natural needs, not wanting to live with the smell in the confined space.

Nobody acknowledged his plea. He sat back down on the floor, leaning on the wall and carried on reciting paragraphs from the Koran to gain faith and comfort.

Gradually, he got used to the routine and learnt to cope with the situation as best he could. He would only know how many days had passed by the delivery of his one meal a day. He began to save the bread and eat a little bit at a time to satisfy his hunger. He spent days in confinement, worried sick about his wife and children, neither of which knew his whereabouts. A few days later the door opened and he was blindfolded, then taken for a walk to stretch his legs. They asked him if he needed to go to the toilet to open his bowel. He appealed to his guards to see somebody. He told them that his wife would die if he didn't go to look after her. They laughed.

'Some people have been here for six months and still haven't been seen to,' he was told. 'You are at the back of the queue so don't expect to be leaving us anytime soon.'

With that they steered him back into his cell and locked the door.

Meanwhile, his wife was informed that Ahmed had been taken for questioning and would join her when he could. She was sensibly motivated by her will to survive for the sake of her children, so decided to be brave and continue to Jordan alone. When she arrived at their hotel, she called me immediately.

She told me that Ahmed had been taken for questioning and appealed for me to help. She was frightened and in severe pain from abdominal swelling. She told me that she was deeply jaundiced, the colour of an orange, because of the liver damage. I told her not to panic and that I would sort her and Ahmed out quickly. She gave me her hotel name and contact number and I immediately rang the British Embassy to explain her situation, and appeal for an urgent approval of her visa.

The man answering the phone was a Jordanian employee of the British Embassy.

'Wait, Doctor,' he said, 'the only person who can help you is the British Councillor. Let me put you through to her because without her this could take a good few days to arrange. A short while later I was put through to an English lady and I began to explain the situation again. Halfway through my explanation, she stopped me.

'Doctor, ask your sister-in-law to come and see me personally now. Can you do that, or shall I send a member of my staff to the hotel?'

Her kindness moved me and I thanked her for her help. I called Huda to tell her to go straight to the Embassy to meet with the Councillor. A couple of hours later Huda was on the phone telling me about how kind and helpful the woman had been; she had approved Huda's visa within thirty minutes.

'I arrive at Heathrow tomorrow,' Huda said.

'Great,' I said to her. 'I will be there. Please be strong and hold on until we meet.'

'There are just two things please, Ismaiel,' she said. 'I can't tolerate the pressure inside my stomach anymore. I feel like it is going to burst and I may stop breathing. My legs are so swollen I doubt they will let me fly in this state. I need to get rid of this fluid. I know when Ahmed taps it for me I feel a lot better. What has happened to Ahmed? Where is he and why was he taken for questioning? Did you manage to speak to him yet?'

With that, she began crying.

'Huda,' I began to lie. 'I spoke to somebody in Iraq and Ahmed had a couple of hour's interrogation before being released. He may be coming to see you when he reorganises his papers and has rearranged his passport, so don't worry. I have also spoken to the children and they are all fine, missing you but coping well.'

I tried to hide my panic and worry about Ahmed and the children but deep down I didn't know if my brother was even alive.

'As far as your stomach fluid is concerned, you should go to the hospital so that they can do it for you,' I said.

'No,' she replied, 'I don't want to see anybody here. I can carry on as I am until I meet you tomorrow in England'.

'Okay,' I said to her, 'do you think you can do it yourself? Did you watch how Ahmed did the tapping for you? It's a matter of sticking the needle into the right side of your belly button. You need to put the needle perpendicular and straight to the skin and then thrust it in until yellowish fluid bursts out of your tummy. You have to sit down or lie on your side. Don't do it whilst you are standing and don't let too much fluid out as this might make you dizzy. Once you are comfortable enough you need to pull the needle out. I could come to Jordan to get you Huda, but that will take more than a day and delay things even more.'

I simply wanted to give her the confidence that I was not only there over the phone but that I could be with her at the drop of a hat.

'No,' she said, with comforting confidence, 'thank you for all the trouble you have gone to and for your support. I think I can do it now. I only have the one needle that Ahmed has used about ten times. Shall I use the same one even though it is not sterile?'

I told her that we weren't in an ideal situation and to put the needle on the cooker to heat it up in the hope that it would sterilise it slightly.

'I will use it,' she said, 'and pray to God to keep me alive to see you and your family, and maybe even get home to see Ahmed and my own children'.

She began sobbing on the other end of the line and I could not hold back my own tears. As I sat there listening to her cry, I wondered how one of the richest countries in the world, with a wealth of oil, could allow its people to suffer in this way. I collected myself and continued talking to her.

'Huda, please keep the line open and talk to me whilst you are puncturing your stomach with the needle. Talk me through every step that you are doing. Can you do that?'

'Of course I can, wait a minute Ismaiel, let me get the needle.'

A minute later she returned and talked me through what she was doing. I guided her through the process, telling her to aim the needle at the bruised entry sites where Ahmed had done it for her.

'Oh my God,' she said, 'the yellow fluid is spurting out of my tummy, about a metre away from the bed. The whole floor is soaking'.

With her pain relieved, she began bitterly laughing, laughing at her misery, laughing at her terminal status, laughing because she was Iraqi, laughing because the rest of the world was sleeping.

It was nice to hear her laugh considering her situation, even if it was only a front. I was glad that she had managed to do it on her own. I told her to lie down for an hour and that I would ring her and check she was okay before going to sleep.

I couldn't sleep at all that night, thinking about how scared she must have been, totally alone in a strange hotel in Jordan, the cancer slowly eating away at her body, wondering exactly where my brother was and if he himself was alive.

The following day, her flight landed at Heathrow airport and I waited anxiously at the terminal, looking out for my beautiful sister-in-law. The last time I saw her in Iraq was in 1990. She had fair hair and light skin with deep blue eyes. She was always well-dressed and tended to her looks.

I didn't recognise the woman that was wheeled towards me at Arrivals that day. The emaciated figure, sunk into the wheelchair, was on her deathbed. I drove her straight to Wolverhampton and contacted the surgeon that knew of her condition, asking him to meet me at the hospital in the private room that we had reserved for her. Mr Williams, the Consultant Surgeon, and I set a management plan for her treatment and agreed that it was going to be palliative management only because the disease was too advanced.

Once Huda had been taken care of, I called my eldest brother, Ibrahim, to ask if he knew where Ahmed was.

'I thought they were with you?' he said. 'They said goodbye to us days ago.'

'Well,' I said, 'Huda is here with me. I have taken her straight to the hospital, but Ahmed was apparently taken in for 'questioning' at the checkpoint and should have returned to Baghdad. Has he not been home?'

Ibrahim was shocked, nobody had seen or heard from Ahmed. I tried to stay calm and told Ibrahim that I would find Ahmed and she should keep everybody there and keep them positive and calm.

'Keep me informed,' Ibrahim said, 'and don't tell the children. They think he's with Huda, so let's keep it that way.

They already know they are losing her. If they find out their dad has disappeared, it will destroy them'.

With the phone lines being tapped, I knew nobody would admit to knowing where Ahmed was. I had to act fast, but didn't know where to start.

I remembered that one of my good friends had become one of the top men within Saddam's circle and was working in 'trade' in Jordan. I knew he was most probably working there undercover. I rang him and he was very friendly and happy to help. He was a good friend when I was in Iraq and I had operated on his own family before, so he knew he owed me the favour. I told him the whole story, simply as I had heard it from Huda. The story was vague and unclear but better than nothing at all.

'Leave it with me, Ismaiel,' he said. 'I will ring you back but give me a few days first. These things, as you know, are very difficult to trace even for us. Everybody I will talk to will deny knowledge of him. I will have to make direct contact with Saddam's inner circle to understand what has happened. I am going back to Iraq in a few days and I will have to ask in person. Be patient, my friend, and I will get back to you with some news as soon as I safely can.'

The days dragged on painfully. As each day passed without news, my hopes of finding him alive diminished. Two weeks later I got a call from my friend in Jordan.

'Ismaiel,' he said, 'I am afraid it is not good news. Your brother has been caught up in a big misunderstanding. He could be rotting in a prison cell or...'

I didn't need or want to hear him finish his sentence.

'Just tell me what you know,' I said.

'Well, Ismaiel, I eventually managed to reach the Director General, Saddam's half-brother, at Al-Amin. Everybody else I asked denied any knowledge of him. I arranged to see the Director at home, with another mutual friend, and he made a few phone calls and came back to me. He told me that your brother is in a cell in solitary confinement in Ramadi Prison. He was handed to them by the checkpoint security guard from Trabeel. There were no papers, no charges and no arrest warrant. They simply took him there as another Ahmed Mohammed Ali. He shouldn't have been taken there and the prison warden had no idea of his presence. The Director of Al-Amin has given instructions for Ahmed to be transferred to Baghdad Headquarters tomorrow and he will be set for an inquest as soon as possible. If there is no connection to the wanted Ahmed Mohammed Ali, then they can release him. But they will not let him go without trial.'

Although grateful for the information, I was sick to the stomach thinking about what Ahmed was going through in the hands of Al-Amin.

Following my friend's phone call, Ahmed was transferred to Al-Amin in Baghdad. He had spent three weeks in solitary confinement and had it not been for my contacts in the government he would never have made it out alive.

Ahmed was blindfolded and taken in a car for over three hours before he was able to sense and hear the echo of the engine from the walls. The car seemed to be going underground on a downward spiral route. He counted about four turns and then the car stopped. He was taken out and two men dragged him through a noisy corridor.

He heard blood-curdling screams and cries for help and suddenly wished that he had been left in his silent cell. After about thirty yards, they stopped and a metal door opened. He was once again un-cuffed and pushed into a room. His blindfold was removed.

He found himself in a room, about four by four metres, crowded with prisoners sitting on blankets on the floor. Including Ahmed, there were seventeen of them in total. They all stood up to welcome him in a hospitable Iraqi manner.

At that time he had not shaved for three weeks and looked many years older than he was. He had not changed his clothes or washed since leaving Babylon with Huda. He was dirty and the smell of his clothes was unbearable. His skin felt like fish scales, yet compared to the other sixteen men in the room he was far better off.

The prisoners began welcoming him one by one and as soon as he sat down the men began to hand him pieces of bread and cold meat from under their blankets, offering Ahmed more than he had eaten in weeks. In one corner of the room there was a sink but no bucket.

The others told him that he would have to train his bowels and bladder to open at a set time every day; the time that they let them out to release their natural needs, like dogs. The crowd in the cell shuffled around to make space for him and one of them passed him a blanket to sit on. They all chatted about different things in life but never about why they were there. They wanted to experience some normality.

Ahmed told them about Huda's illness and her trip to England, and the men held a group prayer for her wellbeing. Ahmed was touched by the sentiment and the kind nature of the poor men surrounding him. He turned to the man next to him and asked how long he had been there.

'Nine months, Sir,' he replied then pointed his finger to an old man in the corner. 'But there is our senior prisoner, he has not left this room for two-and-a-half years other than to open his bowels. Our most recent addition was another Ahmed who was brought in here three months ago.'

After a while there, Ahmed felt that he could trust some of the prisoners and he would whisper in their ears to find out how they had ended up there. Most of the time the response was the same as his own; they didn't know why they were there. They would all pray to God to help them through and to save them from the barbaric cruelty that they had found themselves subject to.

Physically, Ahmed learned to cope with the conditions, but psychologically he was tortured every second of every day. His thoughts of Huda and whether or not she was still alive consumed him and his sanity.

One day, at about what Ahmed had guessed to be noon, a soldier came into the prison cell.

'Who is Ahmed Mohammed Ali?' he shouted.

My brother and two other men stood up.

'Come with me, all of you,' he said.

They were handcuffed and, blindfolded, then led from their prison cell into a long corridor and taken into a lift upstairs. They were dragged out of the lift and forced down another long corridor, at the end of which they were thrown into a room and their blindfolds taken off. They were put in line with fourteen other men who were in as just a miserable state as they were; dirty, exhausted and dishevelled.

Behind a desk at the top of the room, a man in his mid-forties, smartly dressed in a military uniform, shouted to the guards.

'Bring in the bastard,' he said.

A very feeble and weak man in his thirties was dragged into the room by two soldiers, his head hanging and his feet trailing behind him. He looked pale and his pyjama trousers were filthy, his white shirt blood-stained. The man behind the desk stood up and approached him.

'Look you son of a bitch, now we have arrested and brought to you nearly every bloody Ahmed Mohammed Ali in the country and I asked you to identify who it was that you were in talks with in Syria. Who is the one we are looking for? If you don't identify the real Ahmed I will fuck your mother and sister in front of your eyes, right here in this room. Look at these people carefully. I am sick to death with your lack of cooperation.'

He slapped him hard across the face but the poor man never raised his head and continued looking at the floor.

The man, led by the two soldiers who were holding him up, was asked to parade in front of the line-up of men and identify his contact in Syria. It was clear that the man had been severely tortured for weeks.

Ahmed began to worry that he couldn't take any more and would pretend to identify his contact from the line-up. It was very tense as the man walked in front of them one by one, looking into their eyes, deciding whether he would pick that person as his accomplice. When he would move to the next one in the line up a sigh of relief could be heard from the man before.

Eventually the tortured prisoner turned to the big man and said, 'None of them, Sir'.

'Look at them again, fucking bastard,' the officer said with great anger and frustration. 'Find me Ahmed or I will chop you into pieces. I will throw you live into the *Tezab* pond.'

The *Tezab* pond was a concentrated nitric acid pond in which they threw people alive and let them chemically burn to death. The man looked at the line-up again and looked down to the floor, without saying anything to the Director.

'Is it still none of them?'

'No, Sir, not one of them,' the old man answered feebly.

Before they knew what was happening, the Director jumped at him, punching him in the face and kicking him in the loin until he fell to the ground. He then began stamping on his head with his heavy army boots until blood could be seen spurting out.

My brother and the other prisoners remained absolutely still, not wanting to look directly at what was happening. They kept their heads facing straight to the wall, not wanting to catch the eyes of the Director and end up with the same treatment.

When the Director felt that he had done sufficient damage to the man's head, he asked the soldiers to take him out of his sights. The door that Ahmed had come through swung open and they were ushered out of the room one by one. As they were leaving a bodyguard leaned over and whispered something into the ear of the Director.

'Who is Ahmed Mohammed Ali Bhayah?' he shouted.

Ahmed told me that he thought his heart had actually stopped beating. He was convinced in that second that they had decided to choose him as the man's connection in Syria. He didn't know whether to immediately identify himself.

'Who is Ahmed Mohammed Ali Bhayah?' the Chief asked again.

Weakly Ahmed responded, 'I am.'

He felt so drained and physically sick from what he had just witnessed that he didn't want to afford him with the title 'Sir'.

The man looked at Ahmed and then at the soldiers and said, 'Let him go'.

'Go? Go where?' Ahmed said, shocked.

'Have you enjoyed your stay with us?' the Director replied aggressively. 'Would you like to stay longer, or would you prefer to leave? If you don't want to go and see your family you can stay here and we will take good care of you...Get him out, now,' he said, shaking his head in disgust. 'I am tired.'

Ahmed was again cuffed, blindfolded and shoved into the back of a car. After a short drive he felt the warmth of the sunshine fall on his face, the first time that he had been out in daylight for more than two months. The fresh air and heat gave him a burst of energy, a glimpse of hope.

'You must have very influential relatives,' one of the men in the car said. 'His Excellency has ordered to expedite your trial. Most people rot in that prison cell for years without a single person asking for them, let alone the General Director himself.'

The man spoke with tones of disgust and unreasoned hatred in his voice. Ahmed remained silent, not wanting to ruin his chances of being set free. The car stopped, the front passenger got out, flipped the seat forward and let Ahmed out. They uncuffed his hands and removed the blindfold. The car sped away.

Ahmed found himself on a busy road just outside the main building of Al-Amin, the White Palace province of Baghdad.

It was about 6 p.m. on this summer day and this was the first breath of fresh air he had taken. He was dazed and relieved, but soon felt angry. He was angry at the way he had been treated like an animal for two months, angry that he had not been apologised to, angry that his wife had probably died alone, angry that there was nothing he could do to get back that precious time with her if she hadn't.

Ahmed flagged down a taxi in the street and asked him to take him to Huda's family house in Baghdad, promising to pay the fare on arrival, as he had no money on him.

Ahmed was silent for the entire journey, thinking of Huda and his children. Was he going to find her family dressed in black? Who had been by her side if she had died? Tears began to roll down his face as the morbid thoughts ran through his mind.

The taxi pulled up outside Huda's family house and Ahmed got out the car, asking the driver to wait while he got the money. He rang the bell and Huda's father opened the door. He fell to his knees in joy when he realised that he was not dressed in black. Huda was still alive. He went into the house, got some money from his father-in-law and went out to pay the taxi driver. The taxi driver had disappeared after seeing the state that Ahmed had been in. He hadn't wanted to charge him for the fare.

After seeing both our family and Huda's family, Ahmed called me on the phone. I told him that Huda was having treatment in hospital, but that he must come as soon as possible. He got all the necessary papers and cleared his name to avoid any further confusion.

He left Iraq, once again heading for Jordan, five days after being released from prison. He went straight to the British Embassy in Amman, to whom I had sent all the necessary papers, including the medical report outlining Huda's terminal illness, and the humane need for him to be with her.

Unfortunately at the Embassy, he was told that it could take at least a week for his application to be processed, as it needed to be sent to the Home Office in London. Ahmed couldn't afford a week. He had already lost two months with her and I didn't know if she was strong enough to survive a week. I rang the Embassy to explain the appalling situation and appealed for their help. Unfortunately this didn't work.

In 1995, the Conservative government was in power and Mr Rowland was the Home Office Secretary. I rang the Home Office directly and spoke to his secretary, explaining the desperate need for immediate help for Ahmed to come and see his wife, to help to get her back to Iraq before she died.

The secretary told me that the Home Secretary was in Brussels and she would pass an urgent message to him whilst he was there. That evening, I received a call from him directly to my house. He demonstrated extreme and incredible concern and kindness over the whole story.

'I am sorry to hear about you sister-in-law's health problem,' he said. 'Just tell me her husband's name and address in Amman.'

I gave him the name and address for Ahmed in Jordan and the following day at 11 a.m. Ahmed was on his flight to Heathrow.

When he arrived in England, he told us of the extraordinary way he had got his visa. After his initial application when he was told to wait at least a week, he was then contacted by the Embassy during the night and was asked to take his passport in the following day. Within thirty minutes, he was granted the visa.

When he arrived we drove from Heathrow to Wolverhampton, and during the four hour drive he told me the whole story regarding his arrest. Then I updated him on the status of Huda's health. Of course Ahmed, until his release from prison and arrival to England, was completely unaware of my involvement of releasing him from prison. My brother Ibrahim was also unaware, as we couldn't have spoken freely on the phone. They both thought that it was pure luck that he was released.

The medical investigations done on Huda showed the disease to be too advanced to have any hope. Mr Williams, her surgeon, was also a very good friend of mine and at my request he was giving her every possible supportive measure to keep her alive until Ahmed arrived.

We came straight off the M6 motorway and drove to New Cross Hospital in Wolverhampton. It was late in the evening, but the kind nurses allowed a visit.

Ahmed walked into the room where she lay, exhausted and sleeping. Her eyes were sunken and she was emaciated. She looked like a corpse. He realised that she was in the last few days of her life and I could see that he was close to breaking point. Not only had he endured the most horrific two months of imprisonment, but also he had lost such precious time in the final weeks of her life. I left him in the room alone with her to give him freedom to cry.

A while later I walked back into the room to check that he was okay. He was sitting by her side, holding her hand. She was in a deep sleep, partly because of the effect of her liver failure on her brain and partly because of the medication. As we both looked over her in silence, she started to stir and opened her eyes.

'I was dreaming of Ahmed, have you heard from him yet?' she said, looking at me first before noticing Ahmed. The sight of him made her smile instantaneously and with what little energy she had left, she extended a tired hand towards her long lost husband to bring him closer to her.

She was exhausted and I couldn't take any more. I left the room before I became too emotional in front of both of them. I knew I had to be strong for my brother and for his wife, but I felt as if I didn't have any strength left to pretend anymore.

I stood outside the room and I could hear them chatting to each other, both trying to establish some form of normality in their conversation; Ahmed blaming delayed paperwork for his late arrival. Huda insisted on leaving the hospital that night.

She wanted to go home and see her children before it was too late. I spoke to Mr Williams who agreed that she would be allowed to do exactly what she wanted to; although he could not guarantee that she would land in Iraq alive. Wanting to fulfil her final wish, we packed her suitcase and drove to my house where Mary and my children were waiting to see their Uncle. They had not seen him since leaving Iraq. Although the children were very young, they seemed to understand what was happening and it was a very emotional reunion.

Ahmed and Huda spent the whole night catching up. They called their own children in Iraq and spoke to them for hours, reassuring them that everything was okay. They agreed to fly home the following day, but I knew that no airline would accept such a terminally ill passenger on board. Ahmed was desperate to get her back to Iraq, so we would have to disguise how ill she really was.

'Do whatever you can to disguise her illness,' he said. 'If we fail then I will stay here until she dies in England, but I don't want to take the children her dead body. I want them to see her before she dies and I know it will make her very happy to be with them.'

Before leaving for the airport, Mary took to the task of disguising Huda's poor state. She covered her face in heavy make-up, making her cheeks rose red to reflect the glow of a healthy person and disguise her jaundice. Huda had lost almost all of her hair through chemotherapy and Mary covered her head with a hat. She gave her some large, dark sunglasses to hide her sunken eyes.

When we got to Heathrow, Huda was unable to stand or walk, so we put her in a wheelchair and she was pushed by one of the porters to check in. We were very lucky with the helpful and kind-hearted porter who understood the situation and realised how desperately we needed to get her on the aeroplane to see her children. He promised to escort her up to her seat and to make sure that she boarded the flight.

The moment came when we had to kiss them goodbye. It was one of the most heart-wrenching moments of my life, knowing we would never see Huda again and the pain that was to come for them all.

It had been the shortest and most depressing family visit in every way. Ahmed had never even had the chance to change or shower whilst he was in England. He simply came to collect his dying wife, to take her on the twenty-four hour journey back to Iraq.

When I got back from the airport, I called my nieces and nephews to tell them that their mum was on her way back, and that they'd better be waiting for her at their grandparent's house. I prayed that they would be greeting her alive.

When they arrived at her parent's house in Baghdad, Huda apparently felt very alive, as though she had all the strength in the world. She told them the story of her time in England, trying to explain what life was like with my family. They had a lovely meal together cooked by their grandmother. Ahmed said that when he finally looked at the time, it was 12.30 a.m. So he suggested to Huda that they go back to their own house in Hilla and they would have another chat in the morning over breakfast.

When they got home, Huda put her head on a pillow and lay on one of the settees in the sitting room. Her six children put sleeping bags around her and put their heads down for some sleep by their mum.

The only one who stayed awake was Ahmed. Ahmed said he felt strange and didn't sleep that night. He stayed awake, watching over his wife and children and read the Koran to bless them all.

Huda closed her eyes, content that she had seen her children and parents, and most importantly she had Ahmed back safe and sound. Huda died in her sleep that night.

The Mayor of Babylon

In 1984, a new Mayor was appointed in Hilla. He was a ruthless, uneducated and aggressive man. For someone in his position, he had absolutely no professionalism. He was rude when he spoke and had no social or ethical etiquette.

From the first day in his role, he would walk the streets with his bodyguards, abusing his power and position of authority. It was customary in Iraq, when a new Mayor was appointed, for the top officials in the city and the heads of the government departments to host a visit from him to introduce themselves and welcome the Mayor to the city.

I was extremely unhappy about the prospect of visiting him because of his reputation. I was not a member of the Ba'ath Party and I didn't want to be forced to do things against my will. Furthermore, I didn't think it was necessary to introduce myself when I was neither a party member nor a head of department at the hospital.

All of my colleagues went with our Director and Managing Director of Health Services to welcome him. The Head of the Security Directorate at the time was a very good friend of mine and we were extremely close. He knew a lot of inside stories about the Mayor and his background. He advised me as a friend to go and see him and not to make myself stand out from day one. I said that I would go in my own time or wait for a formal occasion to meet him. He wasn't happy with my attitude, warning me that sooner or later I would have to deal with the Mayor and it wouldn't be good if I hadn't made the effort to introduce myself.

Six months later, the Mayor decided to circumcise his five year-old son at our hospital. Friday was our only working day off, our weekend. Most of the celebrated occasions like weddings and circumcisions were held on Thursday nights or Friday mornings.

The Mayor had chosen Friday for his son's operation and he had also chosen a surgeon, who was in charge of the Ba'ath Party organisation in our hospital. The day came round and there was an allocated surgeon and anaesthetist. Our Director was present to oversee the procedure and ensure the Mayor was happy.

However, the day before the operation, towards the end of the working day, we received an order from the Mayor's office to the following effect: 'Master Mohammed, the son of our Mayor, is having his circumcision tomorrow. It has been decided that tomorrow will be an ordinary working day for all medical and nursing staff. Absence or sick leave is not permitted and all staff must be at work by 9 a.m.'

I asked the Director if we were going to do some extra clinics or see some more patients. He told me that the hospital would remain closed to the public, but that we would all need to be present until the Mayor's son was discharged. I was outraged by the waste of time and the fact that our weekend was being taken away from us.

We had all been desperately waiting for Friday to come around, to spend it with our families and children. Instead we were now being ordered to be on standby for a five year-old boy having a minor operation. It was obvious that the Mayor was once again abusing his position and trying to humiliate highly qualified and hard-working academics by making them come to work at the weekend to oversee his child having his prepuce removed.

The more I thought about the order, the angrier I became. I literally could not bring myself to agree to such a ridiculous command. I went to see the Director of the hospital to inform him that I would not be in the following day. I made up an excuse to say that Mary wasn't well and I needed to take her to see a specialist in Baghdad. The Director advised me strongly not to go.

'Don't play with fire Ismaiel, it will not be looked upon well by the Mayor. His office has asked me to open a record of attendance tomorrow and they want me to send it by the end of the day. I can't give you permission not to attend, neither can I take such responsibility. Ismaiel, don't you realise that not only have you not been to introduce yourself but now you plan to ignore his order and stay at home. You are exposing yourself to unnecessary hassle.'

I went home and talked to Mary, who tried to talk me into going to work the following day. I couldn't sleep, I couldn't relax. I was not prepared to go ahead with such an insult. A surgeon and anaesthetist had already been chosen to do the operation and half the nursing staff would be present to support them. I didn't see why I should be giving up my free family time to be an onlooker.

Mary told me to turn up for at least a couple of hours, but I couldn't do it. It was just not in my nature to do something that I could not justify. In the middle of the night, I said to Mary that we should go to Baghdad and stay at the Sheraton. I told her that I would call the Director and tell him that she wasn't feeling well and that we had to leave for Baghdad urgently. We woke up the kids, packed up the car and went to Baghdad to enjoy the weekend.

It turned out that only two consultants didn't attend on that Friday: myself and a consultant urologist. My friend, the Chief of Al-Amin, contacted me. He spoke with real honesty and frustration.

'Ismaiel, you were absent yesterday,' he said. 'What are you playing at? Why are you putting yourself in such a difficult position? You know the Mayor wanted to know why two consultants hadn't attended the operation as ordered. You have put me in a very difficult situation. Everybody knows how close we are, but if I let you off the hook how are we going to handle the urologist? And if I punish the urologist, you must be punished too. Don't push your luck too far with this ruthless man. Go and see him, introduce yourself and explain the reason why you were unable to attend yesterday. We all know that you have got contacts at the top, but remember you are dealing with a relative of the President here. Regardless of your connections this man is influential and strong, I hope you understand.'

I understood perfectly, but didn't regret my decision. I knew though that I now had to think of a way of getting out of this mess without losing my self-respect and pride. More importantly, I wanted to avoid directly apologising to the Mayor. I called to the gold market and bought a nice gold chain for the circumcised boy and a very heavy gold necklace for his mother.

After leaving the jewellers I went to buy a card to express my extreme happiness for the occasion of the Mayor's little boy departing with his foreskin. Of course, I added a compliment for the proud mother of the circumcised. I then rang the Mayor's office and asked his secretary for an appointment. While I was on the line I was told to go in and see him immediately.

Half an hour later I was sat with the Mayor. He was obviously expecting me and was extremely nice and welcoming. He asked me about work and my social life and he made sure to enquire about Mary and how she was after Friday's visit to the Doctor in Baghdad, making me fully aware that my absence was reported.

However, he never directly addressed the issue. When we had finished the usual introductions and phonily friendly chat, I apologised for not visiting him earlier, and also about my unforeseen circumstances that made me absent on Friday's big occasion. Then I reached for the gift boxes and handed them over to him.

'This, as you know, is our custom and I hope you accept it from me. It is a 21-carat gold chain for your dear boy, and there is a place where you can engrave the occasion or his name on it. I chose it because it was masculine and I thought it would be nice on him.'

I then picked up the other box and handed it to him.

'And this one is a simple present from Mary, my wife, to yours. I hope that we will see your family on a social occasion soon.'

It was clear that he was very happy and impressed with the presents, and he shook hands with me, thanking me for coming to see him.

From that meeting on, I became his favourite surgeon and he called on me for all his medical needs. At the time I was blissfully unaware of the sadistic world he was to expose me to.

Unfortunately, the cruelty, which I was forced to witness, scarred me for life.

The Mayor had become very famous for a particular pledge he had made. He vowed to break the hands of anybody who dared to raise them to those who worked for him.

In Hilla, all car mechanics, body shop workers and car accessory shops were gathered in an industrial estate. In Babylon, we didn't have a Mercedes specialist garage but on the industrial estate there were two brothers who were as well-known for their skills as they were for their kindness and fair prices. They used to work on the basis of first come, first served, regardless of who the customer was. This meant that there was always a long queue outside their workshop.

One day the Mayor's own light green Mercedes 280S, dubbed 'the dolphin' needed some mechanical attention. The

Mayor was planning to go to Baghdad. He sent his driver to have the car checked to make sure it was mechanically safe before they set off on the long journey. The Mayor's driver pulled up outside their garage and went over to one of the brothers who was busy repairing a car.

'Come with me and check the Mayor's car, I don't have time to queue.'

The car mechanic knew the Mayor's pledge.

'Okay,' he said, 'just give me a few minutes to finish off this job and I will be with you next.'

'No, it is the Mayor's car and you must come to look at it now. He has to go to Baghdad on a very important business trip. Leave this car and follow me now.'

The car mechanic tried again to explain to the driver that he was in the middle of a very delicate repair and he couldn't leave it half-done. The Mayor's driver grabbed the car mechanic by his wrists and pulled him away from the job he was doing, dragging him towards the Mayor's car.

The Mechanic resisted and tried to free his hands from the driver's grip, but as he did so he hit the corner of the driver's mouth and caused a small cut with some bleeding. The driver, realising he was bleeding from the mouth, became furious People started to gather around.

'You ignorant dogs will be punished,' he shouted. 'Don't you know not to raise a hand to the Mayor's driver? My boss never breaks a promise and I assure you he will make an example of you for the rest of the people in Hilla.'

The driver, with the cut on his lip, got into the car and sped away.

The Hanging Gardens of Babylon

The alleged 'assault' went down as a massive insult to the Mayor's ego. He ordered his bodyguards to contact the Head of Police to pick up the car mechanic and take him straight to the central police department.

It was then that I received a call from the Mayor's secretary. She told me that he wanted me at the hospital within half an hour. I wasn't given the opportunity to provide an excuse so I cancelled my clinic, got into my car, and drove there immediately.

On arrival at the police station, the word had spread amongst the locals, particularly those on the industrial estate: the Mayor was going to punish the car mechanic who had insulted his driver. A huge crowd of people ran towards the police station to see what would happen next, gathering outside the main building and looking through the metal bars of the fence.

The mechanic was being held by police officers in the front courtyard. The Chief of Police, his police officers and the Mayor's bodyguards lined up in their khaki uniforms. To any outside observer, it might seem as if the country was at war. I arrived and greeted the Mayor and his officials and stood in the courtyard with them. I never asked why I had been called there, the Mayor simply asked me to stand next to him in the front line.

'Come here next to me Doctor,' he said. 'I want you to watch what is about to happen to somebody who punched my driver in the face this morning. My driver was very polite and courteous when he took my car for repair, but some people are so full of hatred for us that I have to teach them a lesson. They must know their limits. This animal here will be an example for the rest of the city, so that they understand what happens when you raise your hand to one of my men. I have brought you here Doctor to tell me when his hand is actually broken.'

He said it loud enough for everybody in the courtyard to hear.

'To break his hand, Doctor, means a break, not just a bruise or a fracture,' he continued. 'I want your assurance that at the end of this the bones in his hand will have been completely crushed to a pulp. If you don't tell me the truth my friend, I will hold you personally responsible.'

I wanted to attempt to save the man from such pain and humiliation.

'Sir, why don't you have Al-Amin take care of this for you? You know that they can teach him a good lesson inside a prison cell. I am sure he will never do anything like this again in his life. To torture him in front of people may not do you and the government any good, Sir.'

Secretly, I was also mindful of my own presence at this barbaric gathering. All the people of Hilla were watching me stand next to the Mayor as he was about to publicly torture an innocent man. I didn't want them to think that I was part of his party, nor supportive of his actions.

'Don't worry, Doctor,' he said sensing my apprehension. 'To be with us is much safer for you than being with those riff raff.'

With a nod from the Mayor, the car mechanic was taken out of the police car and escorted by two guards from the Mayor's personal security. A soldier got a metal anvil out of another car and put it on the floor of the car-park, right in front of where the Mayor and I were standing.

Hundreds of people had gathered by now. The entire situation was surreal and barbaric. The car mechanic's hands were un-cuffed and his right forearm was stretched across the metal anvil, held at the elbow and hand by two soldiers.

A third soldier then took a long metal bar, raised it above his head and brought it down right across the man's forearm. The soldier, excited, started repeating this action, beating the man's arm to a pulp in the most savage, cruel and ruthless way. After every hit he looked back at the Mayor with a grin on his face. The Mayor would nod to signal for him to continue.

The mechanic tried to resist from shouting. Instead, he lay still, closed his eyes and appeared unconscious. I have no idea how he tolerated it. With every hammering of his arm, his body shook. After many vicious blows, his arm became hugely swollen and immediately bruised from severe internal bleeding. The Mayor shouted for the soldier to stop, put his hand on my back and leant towards me.

'Doctor, go and examine this animal's arm and assure me that every bone has been broken. If you are not sure, we will continue.'

I didn't have to go over to know that his bones were broken. The Mayor himself must have known that they would have broken with the first hit. I felt as though I was brought in to play a role in a huge and sadistic theatrical display of power.

Taking a deep breath, I headed towards the poor man, with a deep, sick feeling in the pit of my stomach. I knew if I didn't comply I would have a similar fate. As a Doctor I couldn't believe that any human being could physically tolerate such a beating without passing out or screaming in pain.

I squatted next to the man and palpated the area, which by now looked like a macerated, puffed mass of meat. His hand was severely swollen, congested and blue with no pulse at the wrist. He didn't wince or move as I examined the area, most likely because all the nerve endings had been damaged.

'Your Excellency, it has been damaged beyond repair. This man will lose his arm completely,' I said with certainty and assertiveness.

'Dr Ismaiel, you have not assured me if his bones are broken.'

'They have, Sir,' I said. 'They have not only been broken but they have been smashed beyond repair and he will never have the use of his arm again.'

He shouted at the soldiers to take him to a prison cell and spat towards the unconscious man as he did so. He then looked at me and smiled.

'Thank you for coming, Doctor. Tell me how is the Madame and your lovely daughters?'

He had just tortured a man alive and turned to ask me about my family as if we had just watched a play.

'They are well, thank you,' I replied the whole time focussing on the car mechanic from the corner of my eye. 'But may I ask, Sir, can I have your permission to take him to the hospital and call an orthopaedic surgeon to treat this man?'

'No, let the bastard suffer' he responded immediately. 'Let him lose the ignorant hand he raised to my men.'

I had to think quickly to put forward an argument he would understand in order to get the man some help and save him from more torture in a prison cell.

'Sir, I can assure you he will lose his arm. He will never work again and his life has been destroyed. But please, Sir, for my sake, I will be very badly criticised as a Doctor by all your people if I do not call an orthopaedic surgeon. I am sure you don't want to be associated with a Doctor with a poor reputation, sir.'

He looked at me with a satisfied smile, shook my hand and as he got into his waiting car.

'Only for you, Doctor. I will leave you to do your job, I have done mine.'

I called an orthopaedic surgeon who assessed the man in five minutes and decided on his immediate transfer to an orthopaedic hospital in Baghdad. There he was subjected to emergency surgery to release the large blood clots in the arm. After that he underwent multiple staged operations to review and debride the dead tissues.

Eventually, nearly six months later, he had left the hospital with complete loss of function in his right hand. His wife, children and brother decided to go to Baghdad to meet Saddam and complain about the Mayor who was one of his closest relatives.

At the reception of the republican palace, they were met by the chief of his bodyguards; After they explained their grievance, he responded:

'You really are cheeky animals. How dare you come to the President to complain about his judgement? We placed one of the best men as Mayor of Babylon and he did nothing but improve your city and quality of life. Do you really have the nerve to complain?'

Intimidated, they thanked the man for his 'kindness' and left.

The car mechanic continued to go daily to his workshop and advise his brother and son on jobs, as he was never able to do his job again.

The Mayor spent three years in Hilla. He was promoted to a higher position as an advisor to the president at the republican palace. Perhaps he was rewarded for successfully treating the "disloyal animals" in Hilla.

I can safely say that he was the worst human being I ever came across.

Punishment

As Iraq seemed to make more and more enemies, it experienced tremendous pressure and isolation from the international community, from both Arabic and non-Arabic countries.

The deportation of the Shea's to Iran, a war with Iran, the invasion of Kuwait, the extreme and inhumane killing of the Kurds in the north of Iraq and the most ruthless and aggressive handling of the uprising of the Shea's in the south all made the government more strict and suspicious of its own people, in particular the Shea Muslims that constituted the majority.

Any talk or action that might have been interpreted to be against the regime would be ruthlessly punished and oppressed. All Iraqis made a conscious effort not to talk about the government or politics, whether in public or at home. In particular, one had to understand that criticising Saddam in any way, shape or form was a massive risk and was deemed totally unforgivable.

Saddam Hussein and his regime haunted the Iraqi people with constant television appearances. If we turned the TV or radio on at any time of day, we were invariably confronted with a song, programme, interview or news bulletin about Saddam and how great he was.

Whatever he said on television would become law with immediate effect; he didn't need to go through systems and processes and paperwork. One of his many warnings to the Iraqi people was that those who criticised the present regime would have their tongues cut out.

After the invasion of Kuwait, and the subsequent gathering of the American and international forces in the Gulf, Saddam appeared on television talking to the Command Council members. He criticised the Arabic leaders, in particular the Gulf sheiks, for allowing the Americans to have a military presence in the Gulf area.

Saddam thought that to allow foreign soldiers to reside on your land was a great shame and indicated a lack of honour on the part of those governments, especially if they were on holy land such as Mecca in Saudi Arabia.

As the international community, lead by the Americans, were having talks with the Arabic countries, particularly Saudi Arabia, to use their land as a base for the liberation of Kuwait, Saddam began labelling the leaders of the Gulf countries as traitors.

In Arabic countries, a beard or moustache was considered as a sign of masculinity, self-respect and great honour. If a man gave you his word or promise to do something, he touched his moustache or beard to signify his assurance that he would honour his word regardless of the cost. If you wanted to take away a man's honour and humiliate him, you would threaten to shave his moustache or beard to rid them of their respect.

Whilst Saddam was criticizing the Gulf leaders for allowing the Americans to land on their soil, he used an Iraqi Bedouin phrase: 'I wonder how their moustaches did not shake when they allowed this to happen.' The phrase was heard by every Iraqi and became one of Saddam Hussein's most famous sayings.

Around that time, in Hilla, three friends gathered for a private party, one of whom was the host. The men were talking about how another friend had recently been up to no good. One of the men, trying to be witty and humorous, said, 'I wonder how his moustache did not shake when he did it'.

He impersonated the President's phrase and imitated his laugh. One of the other men at the gathering reported his friend to the Party Headquarters for making fun of the President and attempting to impersonate him in an insulting manner.

Within a short time, the story had clearly cascaded to Al-Amin. The culprit was arrested immediately and confessed to his mistake of impersonating Saddam. He expressed his regret and apologised for his comment, explaining that he never meant to insult to President.

All government officers, regardless of their position, were afraid for their own lives when it came to complying with Saddam's order and they would follow them religiously. They cut his tongue out, and it had to be done publicly to send out a strong message to the rest of the country.

A police car and ambulance arrived at a central roundabout near the main police station in the city centre of Hilla. They were quickly surrounded by hundreds of people who had heard of the punishment. Ba'ath Party members with their soldiers and bodyguards soon joined too. It was obligatory for Ba'ath Party members from each government office to be present at such occasions to see first-hand the lesson that should be taught and the message that they ought to cascade.

In front of the crowd, the handcuffed man was forced to his knees and told to put his tongue out. His tongue was held by a piece of gauze to prevent it from slipping back into his mouth, and cut off with a razor sharp knife. They held it up to show the crowd. The man collapsed with pain and heavy bleeding. A Doctor stepped in to resuscitate him and stop the bleeding. They didn't want traitors to die but to suffer as mutes for the rest of their lives.

These cruel and medieval punishments were repeated in various parts of Iraq. People with mutilated bodies, with their ears and tongues removed, were a not infrequent sight in Iraq and to this day are a harsh reminder of the era of Saddam Hussein's dictatorship over the Iraqi people.

08.08.88

The war on Iran ended exactly eight years to the day after it started on 08.08.1988. The immediate reaction in Iraq was of total national celebration.

Iraqis, no matter where they were or what they were doing, ran out into the streets to celebrate in euphoric happiness. Music filled the streets and people were waving the President's photo and Iraqi flags on their cars. Horns were honked and people jumped and danced on the back of lorries and on top of buildings.

There was an astonishing festival of happiness. Life in Iraq suddenly came to an absolute standstill. The supermarkets, offices, schools and banks closed and nobody went to work. The number of celebratory bullets fired in the first few hours of celebration may have been more than in a week of the war. Millions of rounds of ammunition were fired into the air and nobody considered the dangers of a stray bullet landing and killing a fellow Iraqi.

I remember exactly where I was at the time the news was announced. I was in a private clinic and my patients went running out onto the streets, celebrating with the rest of the public.

The happiness of the news had over-ridden the pain of their illness. They forgot about their consultations.

Before I left my clinic, I rang Mary to make sure that her and the kids wouldn't go out into the garden, on the balcony or onto the roof, but as I expected Mary knew full well the dangers involved and had sat the kids in front of the TV to watch the celebrations. She had closed all of the balcony doors to avoid any possible accidents.

It wasn't long before Saddam declared that celebratory gunfire was not permitted because hundreds of people had died instantly and unexpectedly. I remember talking to one of my psychiatric colleagues.

'I feel sorry for those naive people celebrating on the streets,' he said. 'They don't realise that today is the start of the real war for Iraqi people.'

Those were words that I will never forget and which ring true to this day. The Iran/Iraq war may have ended, but it was only then that the social war was to begin.

The mentally and physically disabled soldiers started filling the towns of Iraq. During the war they were hailed as heroes. Many soldiers had been given the honorary title of 'the President's friend', which had given them automatic privileges and social respect. The soldiers were always in the media, radio and television giving personal interviews, talking about their outstanding bravery and contribution.

Very often they were invited to meet with the President, although most public appearances would be with one of his body doubles. There used to be a daily television programme showing Saddam presenting the soldiers with medals and distinction awards. With these medals came free cars, a large sum of money, a piece of land and automatic elite status in society.

Around two million men were actively involved in the war. Now they were forgotten men. Around two million men had now found themselves abandoned. Suddenly and overnight they were in peacetime and didn't know what to do with themselves. They were no longer the centre of attention and no longer Saddam's special friends. The soldiers found it difficult to accept the change and refused to believe that Iraq was to move forward in peace.

Society was not prepared or educated enough at the time to care for physically or mentally disabled people on such a large scale. Suddenly these war heroes found themselves segregated and neglected by the rest of society. The soldiers who survived the war without physical disabilities started to suffer from split personality and other psychological disorders.

They had to somehow adjust to normal day to day civil life, but their minds had been trained for eight years to be killers with no regard for human life. The years that most teenagers would have spent developing a belief system were replaced with brainwashing. We had had eight years of nothing but war broadcast into our homes and now Iraq didn't know how to deal with the consequences.

Iraqis were never allowed satellite television or any form of outside media, to know how the rest of the world was living. Even after the war ended, we felt trapped in a time of war and a time of suffering.

The restless soldiers began behaving extremely violently, and street rage, theft and violence became common, making it unsafe to go out at night. What added to the problem was the abundant availability of weapons and light arms, which became more accessible to the Iraqi people than bread. There were a huge number of illegal and unlicensed weapons sold on the black market; for the Iraqis a gun became an essential household item. Many people, myself included, possessed different types of guns and ammunition on the house. I started to realise that I needed a gun at home to protect my family.

With a British wife and four daughters, I always carried a gun when we went out, one under my jacket and one under the car seat. In my house I had a display unit for the guns; two Sterling automatic guns, two Browning pistols and three automatic shotguns for hunting. Breaking into houses became so common that thieves didn't wait for the house to be empty, they would break in whilst you were sitting having dinner.

Therefore, I felt that guns were essential in the house. I personally felt that I had more of a responsibility than most because Mary had entrusted me with her life by coming to Iraq. I had to protect and look after her as I had promised. I had to honour my vow to her that she would be safe with me in my country.

Having given me four adorable daughters, it was an even heavier burden to protect them all and I was more than prepared to sacrifice my life for their safety.

Thanks to my contacts and good relationship with the local government, I never needed to use the guns and we were always accompanied by bodyguards when we went out at night and at parties.

I mostly used my guns for leisure purposes, especially when we went to my orchard on the Euphrates River. We used to line up cans and bottles along the Euphrates and shoot at them. I tried to teach May, my eldest daughter, to shoot and I remember the first time she held a shotgun in her hand, insisting on firing it herself. She was only eight years-old. I was standing behind her to support her small body but still, when she fired the gun, both of us were thrown on the floor. In spite of the bruise on her shoulder she seemed to be happy using it and knew the dangers of firearms.

To an outsider it was irresponsible, but unless you have lived under such circumstances and watched the country that you loved become a living nightmare, it is hard to understand the extent you would go to protect your loved ones. For me, that included making sure my children could hold a gun and fire it in self defence to protect their mother from harm if it ever came down to it.

My family and I were fortunate in that I had earned myself a privileged status in society, both due to my family background and my reputation as a Doctor. Life for us was good and we didn't live in fear from the chaos around us, but I know many that did.

In our social life, our family and friends were not affected directly by the aftermath of the war and we continued to live an extremely privileged life. That was until in the summer of 1990 when a close friend came to my door and told us that we had to leave Iraq immediately. He refused to tell us why.

I knew that it wasn't a friendly warning. With his help, I obtained a four week holiday from the Minister of Health and also managed to get special permission for my wife and children to travel with me. However, when I came to book the flights, they were all fully booked, with no chance of a flight out of Iraq for a few months. My friend insisted that we were to leave the following day and he was to make sure that we did.

On 30th July, we packed our belongings for a four week holiday. We left the house exactly as anyone would before going away. We were told to show no signs of our intention to leave permanently, but to be honest; we really did not want to leave Iraq forever.

The kid's toys were still out in their rooms, clothes hung in the wardrobe and family photos were left standing on the shelves. The thought of saying goodbye to my family and friends made my stomach churn. I called my brother Ahmed to tell him that we were taking a last minute holiday to visit Mary's family. I tried to make myself believe that that was all it would be, but I had a feeling deep down that this was much more serious than we had anticipated. We would not be coming back. I could not face saying goodbye to anybody face to face, and the next day we were given a lift to Baghdad International Airport by my friend.

He accompanied us through the check-in point without difficulty and staff saluted him as we passed. He went straight into the office of the Colonel who was the Director of the Airport Security Force and took the six tickets that were waiting for us. We were led onto the aeroplane ahead of any other passengers. He assured me that those who had now lost their seats on this flight would be on the next plane out.

He put us in our seats and turned to me, the first and last time I would see such a strong man with tears in his eyes.

'Ismaiel, look after yourself and your family,' he said. 'You will be greatly missed. I hope that one day you will understand why I have urged you to do this.'

Before I managed to respond, perhaps he had noticed my difficulty in saying anything, he kissed my daughters goodbye and left the aircraft. I sat down and closed my eyes, holding back the mix of emotions that had built up inside of me.

Within twenty-four hours, my world had been turned upside down. I was suddenly taken from a happy existence into one that involved leaving behind my country, my family and my friends with nothing but the clothes in our bags and a few dollars in my pocket.

After we landed at Heathrow Airport, we travelled to Mary's parents' house in the West Midlands. I remember walking into their living room and being faced with the breaking news: the boundaries and exit points in Iraq had been closed. The invasion of Kuwait had begun. Another war.

I broke down as I realised the hell that was to come for my country and all the loved ones that I had left behind. It dawned on me immediately that my friend had saved us from the savage closure of the country's boundaries and selflessly stayed behind to deal with the consequences.

Overnight I had gone from being one of the most successful and famous surgeons in Babylon, with a beautiful house, a fleet of cars and family and friends that loved us all to living in a one bedroom flat in Wolverhampton, sleeping on the floor and living off the few dollars that we had managed to bring with us.

I did a few surgical jobs in England on a temporary basis, hoping deep down that I would be able to return to Iraq.

But as each month passed I realised that the problems were not going to be resolved. I knew that I would have to start a life for my family in the UK, to start from scratch and replace everything that we had lost.

Upon my application I was granted the status of a fully trained surgeon by the Royal College of Surgeons in Edinburgh and was validated to apply for a substantive surgical consultancy position in England. After a few short-term consultancy posts in the Midlands and London, I settled at Trafford General Hospital in Manchester in 1997.

I now live in South Manchester in Cheshire, possibly one of my favourite places to live in the UK. After moving to Trafford General Hospital, I was elected as the Divisional Director of Surgery, a position which I held for nearly nine years. I was also granted seven excellence awards for my work and achievements. With the help of my colleagues, I managed to establish a very successful and highly reputed colorectal cancer service at Trafford General Hospital.

Mary remained a stay-at-home mum, bringing up our five children and taking care of our family home and finances. My three eldest daughters, May, Hannah and Nadia, all followed in my footsteps by studying medicine at Manchester Medical

School. They are all fully qualified Doctors, each one of them specialising in different aspects of medicine.

My youngest daughter, Rose, finished law school at Birmingham University and went on to do a Master's degree in Marketing at Cranfield University before taking up a position working for the government.

The youngest member of my family, my son Amir (nicknamed Muzzi since the age of three) has just finished at Manchester Grammar School for Boys attaining an excellent three A's and has been accepted at Birmingham University to study International Business and Communications.

We did our best to settle into this country and embrace the culture. We made superb friends with colleagues, neighbours and distant family friends. Our lifestyle now is a far cry from that which we experienced when we first landed in the UK in 1990, but not a day goes by that we don't remember where we came from.

The children all settled well into a British lifestyle, but had a very Arabic upbringing in the home, reminding them of the culture that they belong to.

I always dream of going back to Iraq, but unfortunately my life is no more my own. It belongs to my large family and it would be extremely selfish to risk it by going back to Iraq with the current terrorist activities.

I continue to live with my hopes and dreams that one day, I may return to my home country, that my children can see the place they were born and that we can see Iraq in all its glory, as we remember it, not as the unrecognisable place of death and destruction portrayed on our television screens today.

the UK, I believe that I am well-placed to give a sensible, personal analysis on the recent events in my home country. This is nothing more than personal opinion, based on my first hand experiences and life in Iraq.

In my opinion Saddam was a very clever person who had studied carefully both the history of Iraq and the nature of the Iraqi people. He came to power in 1968 with a plan in mind. Whether this was his own, or given to him by others, his plan was to achieve full control of the country with an iron fist; to implant fear in every Iraqi.

He learned from Iraq's past that democracy would be difficult to inaugurate and has a tendency to turn to chaos, as proven now. I believe that democracy is a culture, not a political system. Therefore in order to introduce democracy in any of the Middle Eastern countries, it needs to be a very slow and gradual process. A new generation needs to be properly educated; it is too late for those that have already been brainwashed for the past decades.

It was clear from the outset that Saddam was not prepared to attempt building a democracy. He had decided to be the one and only power, destroying any person who threatened his position, in the most brutal manner possible. From the moment he came into power, life changed for every Iraqi person. Before giving my opinion on the American invasion, I think it is important to paint a picture of the world we lived in.

Psychologically speaking, the man had a grandiosity complex. This was clearly reflected in his behaviour and his lifestyle, from the way he accumulated over seventy mansions and palaces to the way he walked and spoke as though he were God.

One of his most famous palaces, which I saw for myself, was called *Al Qadissya Village.* It was comprised of different houses within the palace, each designed to represent a different part of the world. One part of the palace would be full of desert sand and Bedouin tents, while the next simulated the North Pole with artificial snow and freezing temperatures. Saddam even had his own taste of Venice within this palace, with fresh water flowing through the grounds from one room to another.

He and his family could move from one part of the globe to another without leaving the comfort of their home. His grandiosity was further reflected in the way he dressed, his unique cars and in the many millions of pictures and statues that, by law, filled the streets and had to grace the walls of every home in Iraq.

In spite of this extreme narcissism, he also demonstrated a unique and extraordinary talent of seemingly being able to know everything about his people on an individual basis. He regularly visited both the rich and the poor; obviously nothing more than a show for the outside world and the media. He never ate the food that they offered him; he would have a convoy of chefs and a mobile kitchen that would serve up food as if it were the host's. Most of the time, it would be one of his body doubles that did these visits. Even though the whole country could recognise a fake nobody dared to utter their observation.

Saddam never trusted even the closest of his bodyguards and would never make plans in advance. He wanted few others to be aware of his whereabouts. He would wait until he was in his car before telling his driver and convoy the direction that he wanted to go in, sometimes changing his direction at the last minute to an unexpected location. Saddam was the ultimate mysterious moving target; a man that could not be found by his own wife.

His family naturally shared the same attitude and lifestyle, thinking that they owned Iraq and the Iraqi people. His sons, Oday and Qusay, started behaving as if they were the natural future leaders of the country; both brutal thugs in their own right. Iraqis, those who were with or against Saddam, lived their lives with great fear and caution, so as not to fall foul of the government.

There was no such thing as written law; Saddam was the law. You could easily be killed, imprisoned, deported or kidnapped without trial or trace. The fear implanted in the minds of the Iraqis was a deliberate, intelligent act to make people suspicious of each other and to give Saddam ultimate control. It reached a stage that you had to be careful what you said within your own family, for fear of your own family members reporting you in exchange for lavish rewards.

At home, parents had to watch when they said in front of their children, who might innocently repeat their parents' conversations at school. I remember one such case in Hilla; a young child told his teacher that his father hated Saddam for the misery he had caused the Iraqi's. By the time the child had finished school, his father had already vanished.

Iraqis living abroad were no longer safe with assassinations regularly taking place in Kuwait, Lebanon, Jordan, France and England.

The Iraqis were brainwashed by Saddam to know nothing of the outside world and to love nobody but him. Outside media, broadcasting and advertising were controlled personally by Saddam. Nobody was to have access to television channels that he did not own in his own home and nobody was to listen to news stories from the outside world. Nothing could threaten the perfect world that he believed he had created.

The new generation grew up in a different world and for thirty-five years, between 1968 and 2003, most of them knew nothing in life but Saddam. From primary school, children would read stories about Saddam and his family; there were no imaginary children's characters to dream of. Even the curriculum was centred on him, ensuring that he infiltrated the minds of the young and destroyed the minds of the old. It was as thought he genuinely believed himself to be a prophet sent from God, and he would do everything in his power to ensure that every Iraqi understood that.

There was never any opposition or resistance inside Iraq that had a chance to change his regime, even the surrounding Arabic and non-Arabic neighbours feared him. They were all resigned to the fact that Saddam was a ruthless giant, created and supported by the Americans. He was a man that would crush any attempt to overthrow him, whether that came from inside or outside the country.

Under Saddam's regime, I believe the Iraqi people were forced into one of three categories. It has been my experience that depending on which of these you belonged to, your belief system and opinion on the American invasion varies greatly.

The first category was made up of 'the beneficiaries', who were living an unbelievable life of luxury. The majority of them were from a very poor background with poor education, but they were the easiest to educate by the Ba'ath Party and to train with military knowledge. Such people lived privileged lives and anything they wanted would be theirs in a heartbeat. The lifestyle was a reward in return for their devotion and loyalty to the President.

One of our close friends in Iraq taught the thirteen year-old daughter of one of Saddam's closest bodyguards. She would be driven around in a Mercedes and was paid an extortionate amount to teach the young girl. When the young girl passed her end of year exams' Saddam's bodyguard decided to thank her by hiring out the entire building of the Iraqi Fashion House and arranging a private fashion show where models paraded in an array of evening dresses for her to choose from.

She chose a dress and her measurements were immediately taken; the family imported natural silk from France to make it with. The gift was worth over sixty thousands Iraqi Dinar but she could not bring herself to wear it because it was too precious to ruin. She had asked Mary, my wife, whether she was interested in buying it, but unfortunately it was green in colour (Mary has a superstition of the colour green which I will never quite grasp!) and so she refused.

Saddam would round up the men that had failed in civilian life and offer them a lifestyle that most could only dream of. In return he would have an army full of dedicated followers. Hundreds and thousands of young men were chosen by Saddam and his circle and given a life of absolute luxury and positions in society that were unattainable for most. These were the people that eventually started to run Iraqi towns and cities; from banks to government departments. Uneducated and brainwashed men found themselves living like Kings.

These men remain in Iraq, clinging onto the hope that someday they will regain what they have lost through the American invasion. Anybody rewarded by Saddam in this way understandably loved him, adored him and will miss him forever. In their eyes, those who got rid of him were evil criminals and unwelcome invaders.

The second category of people, were those who were distant from the President's circle, very much oppressed and living life as spectators. All they knew was what they saw on the television and heard in the media. They were a mixture of the Shia people in the south, the Kurdish people in the north and significant number of Sunnis who had not accepted his style of ruling.

They had no rights, but a lot of duties placed upon them. They were isolated and denied the freedom of speech and a decent living. They were helpless in contributing to any form of opposition and those of them that attempted to were subjected, with their families, to the most extreme punishments.

The third category was comprised of the politicians and opposition parties living abroad. These people were politically active, but had no means or power to make any change inside Iraq. Their only hope was for a miraculous event to get rid of the dictator and his sons.

In my eyes, the last two categories constitute the majority of the Iraqi people. For those people, there was no light at the end of the tunnel under the control of Saddam Hussein. These people could never have dreamt that one day they would see an Iraq free of the ruthless dictator.

I can simplify the feelings of those that were against Saddam with the following analogy. A prisoner who has wrongly been charged with the death penalty sits in his prison cell day after day, awaiting execution, with no hope of release and no indication of how long the wait will be.

The fear of the unknown and the mental torture of being imprisoned are unbearable. If one day the prisoner hears that there will be an air raid on the town, he would welcome that event whether it resulted in his death or not. For him, it would provide even a glimmer of hope that he could avoid the death penalty.

It is human nature to want freedom, even at a very high price. In a prison cell your intelligence, your mind and your soul are all imprisoned with you, they are useless to you and the rest of the world. Once you are free in body and mind the possibilities are endless and no matter how short-lived the feeling, it is better to die with hope in your mind than to die rotting in a pit.

For the people against Saddam in the last two categories, the hope came to them through the American invasion. I do not have enough space in this book to discuss how or why this happened and I don't plan to enter political discussions.

However, I believe that this war was just like the air raid for the prisoner; it gave hope to the Iraqi people. The possibility of a better life, no matter how small, was enough to lift their spirits and keep their souls alive. Those that were oppressed by Saddam, for the Kurdish in the north of Iraq who suffered mass killings, the action of the Americans was an act of liberation and justice. To the Kurds, the invaders were saviours.

Of course, for the first category of Iraqis, those who benefited tremendously from Saddam, the American invasion was an act of total aggression on a legitimate government. For these people this invasion meant the loss of a luxury lifestyle and power in their country, and these are the people that will not allow peace and rest in Iraq now.

In the eight years since the invasion, the number of Iraqi lives lost has not neared the total of deaths caused under Saddam's regime in one year. Saddam achieved a regime that brainwashed those who followed him and silenced those that did not.

Reaching an agreement on whether the invasion was right or wrong is almost impossible. Right and wrong are relative variables rather than absolute values. Each group within society has their own experiences and beliefs instilled in them which validate their opinions. My only hope is that the Iraqi people begin to accept what has happened as a fact of life beyond their control and they learn to understand and respect each other's experiences and beliefs to rebuild Iraq. The sad reality is that although the future of Iraq is now in their hands, violence seems to be the only language that the opposition in Iraq know how to use.

For Iraq to move on, the opposition must learn to prove themselves to the rest of the world as the civilised and educated people that they are. They must use the language that the rest of the world understands; using sense, reasoning and two-way dialogue. The American and British army's have reached a convincing agreement with the Iraqi government, that the Iraqi army are now capable of working safely and independently. I do believe that the time has come for the West to pull out of Iraq and allow the people the time to fully understand the changes that have occurred in the past seven years. It is only when the forces pull out that the real learning can start and the time has come for Iraq to stand on its own two feet.

Despite the optimism I have, I am fully aware that the invasion of Iraq was not primarily done to liberate the Iraqi people. Saddam was a dictator over the country for more than thirty-five years, destroying and crushing his own people while the Western world stood by and watched. When Saddam decided not to cooperate and when economic times became difficult, all eyes turned to the gold mine lying under Iraqi soil.

I believe that the Americans had a very strategic plan in place and that they knew exactly what the consequences of their actions were going to be, that they never cared about the Iraqi people. The fact that they have been liberated was a mere side-effect of their selfish actions. Now that they have had access to the oil and money in my home country, they do not care much about how the people will cope and rebuild the lives that they have destroyed.

The arguments will continue and people will always look at the past, at who was right and who was wrong. In my eyes, it is a useless and pointless discussion. The invasion happened and Saddam has gone; the reasons behind this are irrelevant now. I believe that the Iraqi people should focus on this opportunity to unite, in spite of their differences, and to work together to rebuild the country that they love, leaving Saddam Hussein for the history books.

Printed in Great Britain
by Amazon.co.uk, Ltd.,
Marston Gate.